FORD MADOX FORD / *From Apprentice to Craftsman*

Ford
Madox
Ford

From Apprentice to Craftsman

Burke

BY CAROL OHMANN

WESLEYAN UNIVERSITY PRESS / *Middletown, Connecticut*

Library of Congress Catalog Card Number: 64-15101
Manufactured in the United States of America
First Edition

To my daughter Sarah Malin Ohmann

Contents

Author's Note

THE present study began some six or seven years ago when I had read only *The Good Soldier* and *Parade's End*. The long list of Ford Madox Ford's other novels seemed to me then to promise more works that would belong, or very nearly so, to similar categories of accomplishment. It was not to be that sort of shopping trip. The many novels Ford wrote before *The Good Soldier* did not prove to be so many gems lurking in some intellectual equivalent of the Flea Market, needing only to be found in order to be admired. The rewards they offered were harder to come by but none the less interesting for that.

In his early career, Ford was a novelist arrested in paradoxes: he wanted to be a moralist but lacked firm ethical principles; he wanted also to write novels of psychological revelation but was compelled to create again and again heroes and heroines whose motives he did not himself initially understand. The novels Ford wrote before *The Good Soldier*, then, promise excellence rather than achieve it. And they themselves comprise a sort of story: a record of slow and difficult moral and psychological discovery wherein the conscious mind of a creator comes eventually to understand and to subdue to art fictional situations that his unconscious mind had, from the beginning, insisted on telling. To trace Ford's development toward mastery of his material is the ambition of the first three chapters of this study. The fourth and fifth chapters mean to show a number of ways in which the concerns and conflicts of Ford's early fiction contribute not only to character and action but to point of view, structure, and style in *The Good Soldier* and *Parade's End.*

I wish to thank Professor Albert J. Guerard, of Stanford University, who, more than any other critic or novelist, has informed my view of fiction and how it is written. It was my good fortune to be his student at Harvard. I am indebted to him, further, for his reading of an early version of this study. I am grateful, too, to Dr. Harold C. Martin, of Harvard University, for his generous attention to the first stages of this manuscript. He gave good advice and I was lucky to have it. The late Wilson Follett gave me encouragement along with a number of practical suggestions for revision. I owe thanks, finally, to my husband, Professor Richard M. Ohmann, of Wesleyan University, who has been from first to last my listener and, unlike John Dowell's, a responsive one.

—C. O.

Portland, Connecticut
January 1964

FORD MADOX FORD / *From Apprentice to Craftsman*

CHAPTER 1

Early Problems

IN *Return to Yesterday* (1931), the third of his four books of memoirs, Ford Madox Ford tells the following anecdote:

> In due course, as they would, [the Shropshire Lad Club of Pittsburgh] decided to do something to make Mr. Housman aware of their admiration. They subscribed therefore for a solid gold laurel wreath and deputed Miss Cather and Miss McClung to carry it to the poet and explain suitably why it was sent. . . . [Miss Cather and Miss McClung] found their way to Hampstead.
>
> A teeny-tweeny maid opened the door of a boarding-house to the extent of a crack large enough to shew her nose. They were inspected by a landlady from an upper landing. At last they were admitted to a parlour. Its principal ornament was an immense, shiny and very cold-looking grand piano.
>
> They waited a long time. At last there appeared the poet. He exclaimed:
>
> "*Oh!* If I had not thought you were my American cousins I would never have seen you," and disappeared.
>
> They laid the solid gold laurel wreath reverently on the grand piano and departed.[1]

After the publication of *Return to Yesterday*, Willa Cather remarked that she would some day write a "careful and accurate" account of

---

1. New York: Liveright, 1932, pp. 330-332; the English edition was published in 1931. Unless otherwise indicated in these notes, the name Ford Madox Ford appears on the title pages of his cited works.

that visit to Housman. She died without having done so, and her biographer E. K. Brown took on the task of correcting Ford. There was indeed, Brown notes, a journey to Housman's rooms, and the poet mistook the American ladies—they were three, not two—for Canadian cousins. But there was no Shropshire Lad Club of Pittsburgh, no laurel wreath, not even a grand piano. And although there was an awkward silence until the third lady, Dorothy Canfield Fisher, hit upon the happy subject of certain corrupt texts, the famous poet certainly did not "disappear."[2]

Ford tells good anecdotes. He cannot be trusted to tell entirely true ones. Like the imaginative guide at the ruins of the abbey of Cluny, he gestures toward the empty air and fills it with places and persons who may or may not have looked or spoken—so. His unreliability and his disregard for consistency are notorious, and they should function as a caveat not only for the literary historian but as well for the critic. The memoirs cannot be accepted at face value. Neither, very often, can Ford's statements about his own fiction.

He was wont, particularly, to speak much too lightly of his apprenticeship as a novelist—to ignore the problems he had writing his early novels, to underrate the relevance of those novels to his later ones, and to lead critical opinion after him piping down valleys of intellectual ease and credulity.[3] Himself and most of his critics apart, Ford was articled to his craft for a time long enough to raise curiosity and invite an inquiry more than casual. He wrote eighteen novels before he produced a work of art; he was less than twenty when he wrote *The Shifting of the Fire* (1892), and he did not begin *The Good Soldier* (1915) until he was forty. As he himself explained the phenomenon, he always knew he could not write good fiction as a young man and he therefore penned his early works "rather listlessly and a little disdainfully" just for practice.[4] Until

2. *Willa Cather: A Critical Biography* (New York: Knopf, 1953), pp. 105-109. This work was completed by Leon Edel.

3. Paul L. Wiley supplies an agreeable exception to this "rule" of credulity in his *Novelist of Three Worlds: Ford Madox Ford* (Syracuse: Syracuse, 1962).

4. *Joseph Conrad: A Personal Remembrance* (London: Duckworth, 1924), p. 175—hereafter cited as *Joseph Conrad*.

he sat down to write *The Good Soldier*, he had "never really tried to put into any novel [. . .] *all* that [he] knew about writing."[5]

It is an appealing picture—that of the artist who in a moment sheds the guise of dilettante and appears full-armed with the weapons of his craft. But it is, of course, unrealistic. It depends on an intuitive conviction of readiness or ripeness; and, contrariwise, it reveals an unduly rational idea of artistic creation—the amateur need merely apply technical knowledge to become a master. The obvious question remains—why did Ford, despite a precocious beginning, require more than two decades to fulfill his promise as a novelist? To attempt to find the answer, or answers, is my chief concern in the first three chapters of this study.

It would take, I admit straightway, an uncritical reader to urge on any other all the fiction Ford wrote before the first war. In their entirety, these are novels for the specialist, whether in the Edwardian period or in Ford himself, or novels for those with long afternoons. And yet, I hope to be impartial in saying that a selective analysis of Ford's apprentice work is of general interest for two reasons. First, because it offers insight into the creative process itself—a dramatic spectacle, as it were, of an artist trying to discover the meaning of the very material his own imagination supplied; and, second, because it contributes to our understanding and appreciation of those later productions we now regard as major works of fiction, *The Good Soldier* and *Parade's End*.

If Ford's own account of his metamorphosis into master is much too casual, it is also provocative. It points the way at least to a few preliminary reasons for his late arrival at maturity. According to the factual record of his works and days, Ford was *not* a youthful dilettante engaging "listlessly" and "disdainfully" in the art of fiction. He was a professional man of letters, committed to a number of creative interests and constrained to write under an increasing

5. "Dedicatory Letter," *The Good Soldier: A Tale of Passion* (New York: Knopf, 1951), p. xviii.

In this book, my omissions from Ford's text are indicated by an ellipsis *in brackets*; any ellipsis not so enclosed is Ford's own. In this usage, I follow the pattern set by Richard A. Cassell in his *Ford Madox Ford: A Study of His Novels* (Baltimore: Johns Hopkins, 1961), p. 32 *et passim*.

burden of financial necessity. Between 1892 and 1913, he published four books of children's stories, six of verse, five of art and literary criticism, four of essays, a biography, a volume of memoirs, a pamphlet on the women's movement—all this apart from his eighteen novels, numerous contributions to periodicals, and a year spent as the first and most distinguished editor of the *English Review*. As the sheer volume of his production shows, Ford wrote quickly; and his early fiction bears obvious marks of haste and carelessness. The syntax is often clumsy, the punctuation erroneous, the diction redundant and imprecise. The following sentence from *Mr. Apollo* (1908) is, unfortunately, typical of many that Ford wrote before the first war:

> For always, when he was at his most triumphant, at his most buoyant—at that moment when he stood more or less genially laughing as on the morning when he had had interviewing him and as it were at his beck and call the secretaries of two members of the Cabinet—he had lurking at the back of his mind and changing his most loud horse-laugh to a sudden quiver, he had that black thought—the fragile veins, the tiny tentacles of his brain that one day—in the very next second perhaps—would give way.[6]

Ford's handling of his narrative is frequently as negligent as his prose. *Mr. Apollo* scores in turn the clergy, the radical intelligentsia, the English system of public education, and the press, and then attempts to unite all these interests under one sweeping prescription of reform: "It is by the worshipping of Gods that men attain to happiness."[7] *The Portrait* (1910), after vacillating between contempt and admiration for a quixotic hero, finally comes lamely to conclusion with the remark that victory is most often "nine parts fortune and one of merit, and so the world goes on."[8] Both *The Simple Life Limited* (1911) and *The New Humpty-Dumpty* (1912), which Ford published under the pseudonym Daniel Chaucer, break from relatively controlled and incisive satire into diffuse melodrama.

---

6. Ford Madox Hueffer, *Mr. Apollo: A Just Possible Story* (London: Methuen, 1908), pp. 245-246.

7. *Ibid.*, p. 309.

8. Ford Madox Hueffer, *The Portrait* (London: Methuen, 1910), p. 307.

Over-productivity, more surely than listlessness and disdain, contributed to Ford's slow development as a novelist. So, probably, did a desire or a need to win commercial success, for many of the early novels, particularly those published after 1908, propound a sentimental ethic. The 'Half Moon' (1909), at least part of The Portrait, The Simple Life Limited, Ladies Whose Bright Eyes (1911), The Panel (1912), and The New Humpty-Dumpty all present heroes who are victims of gratuitous malice. They suffer, or they come perilously close to suffering, extravagant losses—their reputations, their fortunes, the women they love, sometimes even their lives—but they never lose their honor. They cannot, because they are essentially innocent. As the heroine says of the hero in The New Humpty-Dumpty, who may be taken as the apotheosis of this group of heroes, "Count Macdonald [. . .] never thought an unworthy thought and never did an unworthy action. [. . .] I know that he will never do anything that is against my heart."[9]

Many of Ford's early novels, then, do bespeak a lack of effort and a tendency, besides, to simplify character and conflict according to the modes of popular fiction. Yet, as we shall see, the Tudor trilogy is the work of a conscious craftsman who shapes his sentences with care and orders his narrative with calculation, and three novels of contemporary England—The Benefactor (1905), An English Girl (1907), and A Call (1910)—attempt an increasingly subtle exploration of traditional morality. In these works at least, Ford's intentions appear to have been those of a serious novelist. It is true, nonetheless, that the trilogy is tedious and that the novels of modern life, though often impressive, contain stretches of indifferent prose, uncertain tone, and inadequate characterization.

Was it, after all, a disposition to experiment with form, or else a curious reluctance to "put in" his technical knowledge, that blocked Ford from achievement in his early fiction? His success as a novelist, as a brief recollection of The Good Soldier and Parade's End reminds us, was eventually to depend upon a subjective point, or points, of view that would allow him to link

9. Daniel Chaucer, The New Humpty-Dumpty (London & New York: John Lane, 1912), p. 319.

dramatic action by free association, to place it generally in the past, and to speculate freely on its moral import. And his style was to be essentially a spoken style: it would be spare; it would run without complication to its conclusions; it would re-create the diction and rhythms of vigorous, informal speech.

Ford would seem, then, to have been well on the way to artistic fulfillment by the turn of the century. Both *The Inheritors* (1901) and *Romance* (1903), two early novels Ford wrote in collaboration with Conrad, make use of first-person narrators who relate in the present experiences they have lived in the past. Their vision is thus a double and wide-ranging one. They shift back and forth between then and now, ignorance and knowledge, involvement and detachment, as Dowell does in *The Good Soldier*. *The Inheritors*, moreover, offers an early approximation of Ford's later prose, witness the following passage in which the narrator introduces his aunt:

> She was so obviously worn out, so obviously "not what she had been," that her face would have been pitiful but for its immovable expression of class pride. The Grangers of Etchingham, you see, were so absolutely at the top of their own particular kind of tree that it was impossible for them to meet any one who was not an inferior. A man might be a cabinet minister, might even be a prince, but he couldn't be a Granger of Etchingham, couldn't have such an assortment of graves, each containing a Granger, behind his back. The expression didn't even lift for me who had. It couldn't, it was fixed there. One wondered what she was doing in this *galère*. It seemed impossible that she should interest herself in the restoration of the Bourbons—they were all very well, but they weren't even English, let alone a county family. I figured it out that she must have set her own village so much in order that there remained nothing but the setting in order of the rest of the world.[10]

The adverbial intensives, the colloquialisms, the short, decisive periods, all reappear in Ford's mature style. The idiosyncratic tone—the blend of hauteur and irritation, of wonder and an eagerness to

---

10. Joseph Conrad and F. M. Hueffer, *The Inheritors: An Extravagant Story* (Garden City, New York: Doubleday, Page, 1925), p. 113. All subsequent references in the text will be to this edition.

communicate or establish intimacy—also reappears, particularly in *The Good Soldier*.

So far, so good. But after his work with Conrad, Ford's pursuit of technique, if such it was, takes a curious backward turn. In the decade following *The Inheritors* and *Romance*, Ford tries again and again to write "objectively." He entirely neglects the strategy of a first-person point of view, and he relies heavily on the report of a severely detached narrative voice and on the scenic portrayal of dramatic action. He even tends to convey major portions of his narrative in highly formal and mannered discourse. In the Tudor trilogy, with his eye no doubt on Renaissance drama, he develops an artificial poetic rhythm and an archaic vocabulary. He sometimes echoes Henry James in *The Inheritors*. In *The Benefactor* and *An English Girl*, he goes further and fabricates extended areas of Jamesian pastiche. If he was conducting experiments, he had an uncanny instinct for the cultivation of barren pastures.

In retrospect and in the light of one fact further, the whole issue of technique appears to be, like Ford's over-productivity and his suit for popularity, only a secondary cause of his slow development—a diversionary action fought while he grouped his major forces for combat elsewhere. The one fact further is that even when Ford does, in the decade following his collaboration with Conrad, anticipate his later methods, he does not always anticipate them to good effect. When he moves into the mind of one of his characters, he writes well more often than not. But a crucial shift into the mind of the hero at the end of *The Benefactor* results in some of the most abstract and obscure passages in the book, and a similar shift in *A Call* elicits a series of constructions as awkward as any he ever composed. Point of view offers no *certain* index to success or failure. Neither does a departure from orthodox chronology. In *The Portrait*, Ford occasionally effects a shift in time, thereby adding a measure of suspense to his narrative; but he never achieves the significant juxtaposition of event that distinguishes both *The Good Soldier* and *Parade's End*. And at the end of *The Young Lovell* (1913), a whole series of time shifts contributes nothing to the narrative but confusion.

A study of technique, it appears, is not always rewarding in Ford's early fiction. Ford had, certainly, to discover and use a successful structure and style. But he had, just as certainly, to discover a combination of character and conflict that would appeal to his imagination and at the same time allow him to convey a coherent and profound evaluation of human experience. The primary difficulty he faced as a beginning novelist was not, I think, the search for form but the search for content.

The nature of Ford's struggle for material emerges in a rough way in his first and very youthful novel. Conrad read *The Shifting of the Fire*, some years after its publication, and called it " 'delightfully' young, not 'drearily or morally or sadly or frightfully or any of these things which politeness would have induced me to paraphrase.' "[11] The reviewer for the *Athenaeum* had taken a more sober view of it. He regretted that Mr. Hueffer—Ford did not change his name until after the first war—had "chosen for his motive a singularly repellent situation" and "spared no pains to elaborate its hideous incongruity."[12] Although they are at odds, both opinions are relevant; taken together, they point toward the essential character of the novel, and its essential failure. *The Shifting of the Fire* is an uneasy combination of two disparate modes of composition, satire and melodrama.

Among its incidents, the novel includes a grotesque May and January marriage, a near-suicide, and three examples of sudden death, one of them an apparent murder. On the one hand, Ford works to involve us in a sensational story. On the other, he pursues a contrary goal. He repeatedly interrupts his narrative to speak directly to us, to satirize his own characters and the literary taste of his time. The satirical intrusions check our participation in the melodrama. And more, because of their precise and peculiar tone, the tone heard, for example, in the following passage:

> No doubt, dear reader, you will turn up your critical nose, which has grown of late accustomed more to realism than sentimentalism in literature, at the thought of an old maid having need to dry her eyes at the reminiscences of the *temps jadis*

11. Douglas Goldring, *The Last Pre-Raphaelite: A Record of the Life and Writings of Ford Madox Ford* (London: Macdonald, 1948), p. 69. Published in the United States as *Trained for Genius* (New York: Dutton, 1949).

12. *Athenaeum*, No. 3395 (Nov. 19, 1892), p. 700.

which is over and fled half a century ago. But Miss Hallbyne had once been young, and once had been beautiful, and in recollections a day is the same as a thousand years, and 'a thousand years but as a span,' *pour ainsi dire*, and the sight of Hollebone had touched a hidden spring in a ghost closet that contained many and many a faded and dusty note of memory. For Miss Hallbyne had been the less beautiful of two beautiful sisters.[13]

Here Ford busies himself with a traditional function of the intrusive author, looking into the heart of one of his characters and counseling a response to what he finds there. Having established a confidential relationship with us by assuming that we, too, know realistic fiction and will share his dislike for its clinical detachment, he proceeds to explain and apologize for his own character's feelings. In effect, he sues for sympathy on her behalf. But he receives very little because his pose of superiority sets us at a distance. His self-conscious and arch indulgence in clever phrase-making dissipates our attention. If he affects indifference to his main points, we have no choice save to follow his example.

Even when, in *The Shifting of the Fire*, Ford presumes to strip the mask from society and show that an apparently devoted niece really prays for the death of her aunt or that a publicly benevolent husband privately tortures his wife, he speaks with the same light unconcern. His voice is sometimes amusing, but it continually denies importance to what it says. Cupidity and malice do not really matter in a world of trivial or incidental humor. Ford not only cuts his melodrama by his satire: he draws the teeth of his satire by his tone, finally involving us neither emotionally nor intellectually in his novel. And, significantly, his technical difficulties seem to reflect an uncertain conception of the meaning of his material. His alternation between melodrama and satire and his final disposition to unconcern go hand in hand with a contradiction in his moral attitude.

Ford's heroine, Edith Ryland, is very much in love with her fiancé, Clement Hollebone. Her love for Clem, in fact, is all Edith

---

13. H. Ford Hueffer, *The Shifting of the Fire* (London: Unwin, 1892), p. 71. All subsequent references to this novel will appear in the text.

values at the outset of the novel and in her eyes justifies what she subsequently does. When Clem loses his fortune, Edith fakes affection for the septuagenarian Kasker-Ryves and marries him on account of his wealth—not because she cares for money per se but because money will someday reunite her with Clem. She views her mercenary marriage as a noble deed, a heroic sacrifice in the service of love. Even though Kasker-Ryves himself is also guilty of hypocrisy (and a host of other cruelties that render Edith's deception relatively pale), Edith finally decides that she has acted unethically. In an emotional scene, she admits she has wronged her husband and begs his forgiveness. She no longer believes that her love for Clem justifies her marriage to another man; she gives up, in effect, her original standard of all for love to embrace a new standard of honesty and respect for the individual. There seems little doubt from the immediate context of the scene that Ford represents Edith's repentance as sincere and approves of it.

But he grants approval to his hero on other grounds. Although Clem continues to love Edith after Kasker-Ryves' death, he hesitates to propose again because he believes, mistakenly, that she has murdered her husband. Then he receives an unequivocal counsel to action from a friend. Julia begins by reminding him that he gave Edith an opportunity to withdraw from her engagement to him when he lost his fortune and continues with the following:

> You did it in order to vaunt your honourable character, to flatter your own vanity, in fact, by proving to yourself what a very honourable gentleman you were. And you left her to herself, to pine with a half broken heart, instead of coming to comfort her in spite of her parents. That is your honour again. And then in her great chivalrous love she sacrifices herself to gain money for you—and you, instead of wondering at her love, so far above your own, your petty vanity is wounded, and you scorn her and taunt her until, in despair at your hardness of heart, she murders her senile, villainous husband. What other woman would have had the courage? (p. 302).

Here Ford interrupts to question the moral standard expressed—it is, of course, precisely Edith's first one—but so facetiously and so archly that the effect is to mock those who would mock the standard rather than the standard itself. And he voices no other dissent. Clem accepts both Julia's criticism and her challenge. He marries the woman he supposes a murderess. His friends applaud him among themselves and even Edith, who should presumably know better by this time, reverts to her initial unenlightenment and exclaims: "Oh, Clem, how glad I am, how glad I am! I don't think even *I* love you as well as that. I don't think I could have married you if I thought you had committed a murder" (p. 321).

The unmistakable impression is that Ford has contradicted himself. The major part of his novel seems designed to criticize love as an ultimate value, the conclusion to uphold it. Even if his objection to Julia's advice could be construed as fundamentally serious, the facetious tone in which he makes it would reduce the chief conflict of the novel to insignificance. It is true, again, that Ford wrote *The Shifting of the Fire* when he was very young, and to examine it is to take him at a plain disadvantage. Yet the examination is fruitful because the primary fault this first novel displays is essentially typical. The same vacillation in moral attitude appears in much of Ford's early fiction, even, in subtler guise, under the watchful eyes of Conrad in *The Inheritors*.

Of the two novels Ford and Conrad wrote together, *Romance* is the better book. Nothing in *The Inheritors* equals the narrative or descriptive power of Conrad's extensive contributions to *Romance*—the escape of the hero and heroine from a Cuban port and their siege thereafter in a cave surrounded by pirates. But in certain ways *The Inheritors* is the more profound book. It is also the more interesting to the student of Ford because Ford wrote most of it and because, to a degree greater than *Romance*, it bears on the problems of his apprenticeship.[14]

---

14. Ford supplied the plot for *The Inheritors* and wrote almost all of it. Besides making minor contributions to the writing, however, Conrad did attend as critic on the composition of the whole. He confided, in fact, to Edward Garnett that he "made" Ford write every chapter at least twice, most of them three times over (*Letters from Joseph Conrad, 1895-1924*, ed. Edward Garnett [Indianapolis: Bobbs-Merrill, 1928], p. 168), and it is tempting to guess that, but for Conrad's supervision, *The Inheritors* might contain more, and more extensive, contradictions than it does.

Two summaries by Conrad of his contributions are quoted in *The Richard Curle Conrad Collection* (New York: American Art Association,

In its main outline, *The Inheritors* leads its hero to a crucial moral decision. At the climax of the novel, the narrator, Etchingham Granger, has to choose between a purely personal loyalty to the woman he loves and a public loyalty to traditional moral values. He chooses the former, and the consequences are literally nationwide. The English foreign minister, who has always defended traditional morality, is suddenly revealed as the champion of a vicious scheme of colonial exploitation although he is not, in fact, corrupt. He has supported the colonial scheme in the mistaken belief that it was a philanthropic venture, an experiment to form a model state. But the public does not trifle with fine distinctions. The minister is completely discredited and with him the ideals he symbolized. His power passes into the hands of another party whose only principle is self-interest, and a new political era begins. The satirical burden of the novel is the revelation of the ways in which corruption battens on probity and assumes the aspect of the truth it destroys.

Conrad called *The Inheritors* "a sort of skit" on a contemporary type of political novel.[15] The novel seems to reflect, particularly, the influence of H. G. Wells. The men whom the title describes come from an extra-worldly race and, like Ostrog the "Over-man" in *When the Sleeper Wakes* (1899), they scorn earthly feelings and scruples. In Wellsian fashion, they are shaped primarily to illustrate a thesis—their dogmatic function hinders their individual development. But the relationship between the narrator and the heroine, more intricately drawn, adds an interesting measure of subtlety to an otherwise slight performance.

As the action begins, the narrator has just made a resolution to "live," and he is in a holiday mood when he first meets the heroine. She strikes him as warm and vital, an incarnation of the more abundant existence he wants to enjoy, and he repeatedly describes her in terms of light. Yet hers is a distinctive light and the origin of her beauty is curious. She is, as she says, one of the "inheritors." She comes from another dimension, without beliefs, without traditions, without feelings. She therefore represents a beauty that lies

---

1927), Items 40 and 41. Ford commented on the division of the collaboration in his *Joseph Conrad* (p. 134).

15. *Letters from Conrad*, p. 168.

beyond reality and a state of mind that transcends the demands of human morality and passion.

Even at the first meeting, there is a suggestion that the heroine's vitality is deceptive, that she promises death instead of life. Kissing her hand only to find it chill rather than warm, the narrator feels himself threatened with "unknown entanglement" (p. 14). Nonetheless, his preoccupation with her grows. Whereas he first regards her as a part of life, which he thinks he wants to enjoy, he later separates her from the rest of the world and realizes that he desires her presence alone. In an effort to win her by co-operating with her political aims, he reveals the colonial scandal and brings the "inheritors" to power. With his betrayal of his human fellows, he feels that he has passed a personal crisis and achieved some sort of psychic release:

> A feeling of entire tranquillity had come over me. I rested after a strife which had issued in a victory whose meaning was too great to comprehend and enjoy at once. I only knew that it was great because there seemed nothing more left to do. Everything reposed within me—even conscience, even memory, reposed as in death. I had risen above them, and my thoughts moved serenely as in a new light, as men move in sunshine above the graves of the forgotten dead (p. 192).

Only later does he learn that his sense of victory is premature. Despite his co-operation with the heroine, he fails to win her. Still, his failure does not affect his love. As the novel ends with his last meeting with the heroine, he remains convinced of her "beauty" and "glory" (p. 211).

The narrator of *The Inheritors* never fully understands himself. But his habitual metaphors of repose and transcendence, and a number of his actions besides, tell us that he loves the heroine's true nature rather than her apparent one. His attraction to her has really been an unconscious drive—not toward life—but away from it. In pursuing the girl from another dimension, he has attempted no less than to liberate himself from the human condition and all its responsibilities. Yet the moral meaning of his final choice, his preference of the heroine over his traditional obligations, is not untroubled by contradiction.

The relationship between the heroine and the narrator undergoes an interesting change part way through *The Inheritors*. Realizing that, of all the world, the heroine alone attracts him, the narrator follows her to Paris. He is agitated and elated at his arrival in the city, the entrance, as he thinks, to a "better sort of paradise" (p. 93). Then his mood alters abruptly. While the heroine has previously stimulated him, her presence now depresses and paralyzes him. He visits her with reluctance, habitually visualizing her surroundings in terms of death; and when he finally comes to live, with due propriety, beneath the same roof with her, he feels both intensely solitary and deprived of the capacity for action. "When I look back at that time," he says in summary, "I figure myself as forever sitting with uplifted pen, waiting for a word that would not come, and that I did not much care about getting" (p. 133).

The text picks up one of the many implications of his experience and, for a time, pursues it in a way that nearly overturns the moral judgments made elsewhere in the novel. Coincident with the narrator's change from excitement to depression is a change in the heroine herself. Although she says at the beginning that she has no feelings, she admits that living in the world will diminish her resistance to emotion. She will contract emotion as human beings contract disease. By the time she and the narrator meet in Paris, her prediction has come true: she has learned to care for the narrator. And he responds immediately with diffidence and anxiety. When earlier the heroine showed no affection for him, he was able to exclaim confidently, "I wanted to make love to her" (p. 29). Now he sees himself as inadequate:

> I was forever screwing my courage up and feeling it die away. We used to drive about in a coupé, a thing that shut us inexorably together, but which quite as inexorably destroyed all opportunities for what one calls making love. In smooth streets its motion was too glib, on the *pavé* it rattled too abominably. I wanted to make love to her—oh, immensely, but I was never in the mood, or the opportunity was never forthcoming (p. 135).

When he finally manages to declare himself, which he does at the end of the Parisian episode, the heroine rebukes him: " 'Oh, be quiet,' she said at last. 'Be quiet! If you had wanted me I have been here. It is too late. All these days; all these—.' " He has no rejoinder. And then, significantly, "someone opened the great shutters of the windows, and the light from the outside world burst in upon us" (p. 154).

True, the hero's motive remains essentially the same. He is still guided by a wish to escape from life and the responsibilities it entails. But the scene is virtually his last with the heroine before he makes his momentous moral choice: it is the last meeting he describes before deciding to reveal the colonial scandal. The heroine remains in our minds at least as a woman who extends a tacit invitation to engage in human experience and resents the narrator's reluctance to accept it. She is illumined no longer by her own distinctive light but by the light of the real world. Psychologically, her change and the hero's response to it are admirably developed, and the Parisian episode contains some of the best writing in the book. But the heroine's altered symbolic role now casts doubt on the meaning of the hero's moral decision. He still betrays his comrades. He still injures the traditional moral code. But does he not assert his humanity in choosing the course he thinks will win the heroine? Does he not cut himself adrift from one part of the human community only to join with another?

This line of interpretation cannot be developed further. When the heroine returns after the Parisian episode, she resumes her original symbolic function. The narrator's preference for her clearly signifies a break with humanity, a spiritual death. Only a trace of confusing ambiguity appears perhaps in the heroine's last dismissal of the narrator, when she condemns him for indulging in love, which she might well do as a visitant from an extra-human dimension, but then goes on, in lines that clearly recall Julia's exhortation to Clement Hollebone, to criticize him for having loved egoistically rather than generously.

The crux of the difficulty here is an indecisive moral attitude. The prevailing values of *The Inheritors* are clear—the novel grants the attractions of the heroine but disapproves of them; irresponsibility and escape from the human community, however desirable, are finally censured. But in the Parisian episode there is a recognizable tendency to destroy these values and to replace them with their opposites, to disapprove of the narrator's temporary inability to express his love for the heroine and to applaud by extension his final pursuit of her as a difficult and courageous commitment. In the first instance, the way to ease of conscience is broad, common, and prosaic; in the second, it is wholly private, open only to the few who seek a finer existence than that society offers.

It is true, as two recent major contributions to Conrad criticism make clear, that certain striking parallels may reasonably be drawn between *The Inheritors* and Conrad's independent novels. As Thomas Moser has pointed out in his *Joseph Conrad: Achievement and Decline*, the prime motive of Conrad's characters is egoism, and that egoism frequently takes the form of a persistent desire to escape from reality. Man seeks "more profoundly than power and glory—irresponsibility, peace, even death itself."[16] And Albert J. Guerard in *Conrad the Novelist* shows that Conrad not only repeatedly created rebels and outlaws from society, but presented them with profound sympathy.[17] Thus, in its sympathetic treatment of the narrator's motive, *The Inheritors* bears marked resemblances to many of Conrad's works. But to sympathize is not necessarily to approve. In Conrad's world, fidelity to the community remains the ultimate good, infidelity the ultimate crime. In *Lord Jim* alone, the French lieutenant, Stanton, Tamb' Itam, the Malayan helmsmen, the *Patna*'s cooks, and possibly even the *Patna*'s pilgrims all typify stoic devotion to duty. It would be atypical for Conrad to imply sanction of the narrator's choice in *The Inheritors*.[18]

---

16. Cambridge, Mass.: Harvard, 1957, p. 34.

17. Cambridge, Mass.: Harvard, 1958, pp. 1-59 *et passim*.

18. Similarly, the relationship between the narrator and the heroine of *The Inheritors* shows certain resemblances to Conrad's habitual treatment of love. Conrad's heroines, for example, in *Almayer's Folly* and *An Outcast of the Islands* and "The Lagoon" are also associated with death, and in their presence his heroes also experience feelings of inadequacy (Moser, pp. 52-58, 70). But again, the love relationship of *The Inheritors* is more typically Ford's than Conrad's. To begin with, the love story calls forth some of the best writing in the book; and, as Moser has already proven (pp. 50-130), although Conrad often chose to write about love, he almost never did it well, whereas Ford was eventually to do it very well. The heroine, moreover, is not essentially Conradian in character. Her domain is not the European or tropical house or garden; her stage is the world, and her business the fate of nations. In her austerity, her athleticism, and, above all, in her independence, she differs from the usual Conradian woman and foreshadows a number of heroines whom Ford was subsequently to create. Last, as I have shown, the

Comparison with *The Shifting of the Fire*, however, suggests that such a commitment may have been typical for Ford. *The Shifting of the Fire* may be viewed as more than a love story. The characters in the book are divided into two camps—the old and the young. With perhaps one exception, the old people are all presented as disagreeable. They iterate unromantic precepts to the young—one should not, for example, marry without an adequate income—and they demand such tiresome responses from them as reverence, obedience, and devotion to hard work. They exemplify, in short, many traditional Victorian values, and the young are disposed to rebel against them. In *The Shifting of the Fire*, then, Ford created a conflict between two moralities, one social and prosaic, the other purely personal and romantic, and was apparently unable to decide between them, since he approved them both in turn.

I suggested earlier that Ford's foremost problem as a beginning novelist was his search for content. But even this explanation of his long years of apprenticeship doesn't prove to be a simple one. As Caroline Gordon has observed, all of Ford's novels are "part of one story" because he had "only one story to tell."[19] And he discovered that story—or rather, he discovered one of two main variations of it—in the first novels he published. In both *The Shifting of the Fire* and *The Inheritors*, a hero who prides himself on his honor falls in love with a strong-willed and unconventional heroine. If the hero is faithful to the heroine, he must betray his traditional code of moral values. If he is faithful to his code, he must betray the heroine. Except in the youthful *Shifting of the Fire*, he cannot escape his dilemma in possession either of happiness or of ease of conscience.

Honor and love, fidelity and betrayal, innocence and guilt were to appeal to Ford's imagination until the end of his career. In all

suggestion is implicit in *The Inheritors* that the narrator's union with the heroine would be desirable, either emotionally or morally. It would be, in part at least, an occasion not for implicit commiseration, as it is in *Almayer's Folly*, but for congratulation, as it is in *Parade's End*.

19. "The Story of Ford Madox Ford" in *Highlights of Modern Literature*, ed. Francis Brown (New York: New American Library, 1954), p. 117.

his serious novels, he would exploit as a major source of tension the contrary attractions of passion and convention, of individualism and collective responsibility. In a number of his serious novels, he would re-create hesitant heroes like Clement Hollebone in *The Shifting of the Fire* and the narrator of *The Inheritors*. Indeed, the narrator of *The Inheritors* initiates a line of idealistic protagonists who continue to pursue impossible aims in love and who culminate eventually in John Dowell in *The Good Soldier*. Etchingham Granger speaks at times with Dowell's characteristic intonations, and his ambivalent attitude toward the girl from another dimension unmistakably foreshadows Dowell's even more reluctant relationships with Florence Hurlbird, Leonora Ashburnham, and Nancy Rufford.

And yet, despite these quite early anticipations of later character and conflict, Ford still had much to learn about his "story." While *The Inheritors* offers some agreeably subtle and convincing scenes of interaction between hero and heroine, their given situation is, after all, a fantastic one. The heroine's coldness derives simply from her otherworldly origin, the birth of her passion from a change in residence. Again, her final invincibility may be referred to her extraordinary nature, as in part may the narrator's sense that she is sinister and threatening. At many points, the unrealistic terms of the novel's plot serve as substitutes for sustained psychological development. When the narrator remarks, of the political intrigue, that "The whole thing was a matter of under-currents that never came to the surface" (p. 142), he might with equal justice have applied his comment to his relationship with the heroine. The pattern of *The Good Soldier* is there in *The Inheritors*, but dimly conceived and insufficiently realized. In brief, by 1901, Ford knew more or less what happened in the first version of his "story," but he did not know precisely why it happened and he did not know how to interpret it.

Before he could write good fiction, Ford had to carry out two main lines of inquiry. He had to return to and resolve in his own way, rather than Conrad's conservative one, the conflicting moral attitudes of *The Shifting of the Fire* and *The Inheritors*. And he had to explore the characters of his heroes and heroines. He had to determine where, in the phrase from *The Inheritors*, their "better paradise" really lay and why, if it lay in one direction, they should so persistently seek it in another. At a glance, the ethical inquiry might seem to require no more than an exercise in logic. But for Ford the novelist its outcome seems to have been contingent upon the psychological inquiry. Ford, in other words, would not finally know how to judge the conduct of his heroes and heroines until he understood their motives.

CHAPTER 2

Easy Answers

To SEPARATE, as I propose to do here, Ford's historical romances from his novels of contemporary life may well appear an unproductive exercise, likely to draw attention to superficial and largely irrelevant matters. Insofar as any historical novel presents a discernible attitude toward experience, it is, I admit, not merely historical but also contemporary or timeless. George Eliot's urgent insistence on the individual's responsibility to society appears in both *Romola* and *Middlemarch*, and Dickens did not turn aside the general flood of destruction in *The Tale of Two Cities* any more than he dispersed the fog of *Bleak House*. The novelist usually creates similar conflicts and draws parallel conclusions, whether he lays his scene in Renaissance Florence or eighteenth-century Paris or in a time and place he himself knows.

But despite the fact that all the fiction Ford published between *The Inheritors* and *The Good Soldier* displays common interests, a division on the basis of setting is not without consequence. In Ford's early work differences in setting are closely related to differences in accomplishment. With one exception for each genre, the historical romances are more controlled than the novels of contemporary life.[1]

---

1. *The Portrait* is less controlled than the rest of the romances. Its hero confronts the physical and mental ills of the lower classes in a long interlude whose somber tone is incongruous with the main plot, which traces the development of an elaborate eighteenth-century wager. *The Panel: A Sheer Comedy* (published, with revisions, as *Ring for Nancy: A Sheer Comedy* in the United States) possesses narrative unity, although it is a bedroom farce and the slightest and least ambitious of Ford's novels of contemporary scene.

Even when their technique is generally unsuccessful, as it is in the Tudor trilogy, the romances at least have the virtue of narrative unity. Unlike the modern love stories and satires, they are relatively free from interruption and digression, and they do not hesitate to make decisive, if not always consistent, judgments. They therefore show in relief moral attitudes that are often obscure in the novels of contemporary life. At the beginning of the pre-war decade, the romances testify to a recurrence of the conflicts that divide *The Shifting of the Fire* and *The Inheritors*. At the end of the decade, they give evidence of a significant evolution in ethical point of view.

The three volumes of Ford's Tudor trilogy—*The Fifth Queen* (1906), *Privy Seal* (1907), and *The Fifth Queen Crowned* (1908)— enjoy a favored position in Ford's early canon. They have been widely praised, for their interesting historical detail, their exciting narrative, and their vivid characterization. Walter Allen, for example, writes that "Ford liberates his characters [in the trilogy] from the associations encrusting them from four centuries of bitter sectarian history, so that they live as human beings."[2] Kenneth Young agrees, saying, "It is as though history had been wired for television."[3] Richard A. Cassell finds the trilogy a "totally successful attempt to fuse a romantic, idealized character with a realistic method."[4] Paul L. Wiley sees *The Fifth Queen* in particular as approaching "the tone and pattern of mature psychological fiction."[5]

In fact, however, the trilogy bears little resemblance to its representation in criticism. It is not a robust re-creation of either its period or its personages. Nor does it possess the narrative energy that usually characterizes popular historical novels. On the contrary, it is the work of a conscientious but uninspired craftsman who chooses an uncongenial medium and finally fails to explore his subject.

In the three volumes that follow the courtly career of Katharine

2. *The English Novel: A Short Critical History* (London: Phoenix House, 1957), p. 315.

3. *Ford Madox Ford, Bibliographical Series of Supplements to 'British Book News': Writers and Their Work*, No. 74 (London: Longmans, Green, 1956), p. 23.

4. *Ford Madox Ford*, p. 130.

5. *Novelist of Three Worlds*, p. 110.

Howard, Ford confines himself almost entirely to an objective point of view. He discovers his characters on stage and describes them and their setting in detail. (Influenced by his Pre-Raphaelite heritage, he wants to make us see—Tudor forests, parks, riverways, roads, castles, chapels, tennis courts, shops, inns, cottages, bedsteads, tapestries, manuscripts, wines, roast pigs, and pasties.) Then he records present action. He seldom moves into the minds of his characters and he rarely telescopes events by means of summary. His action develops slowly, as it must in any novel that relies heavily on dramatic portrayal. In *The Fifth Queen*, Katharine's enemies plot to destroy her by impugning her chastity. In *Privy Seal*, they try again. In *The Fifth Queen Crowned*, they finally succeed. There are other events, of course. But the central narrative follows an unimaginative line of plot and counterplot, accusation and denial: the development is monotonous as well as slow.

The prose of the trilogy contributes to the over-all impression of stasis. Ford works out two distinct modes of expression, one for narrative, one for direct discourse. The narrative voice, at least, suggests good work to come. It speaks with detachment, sketching background and relating action, implying value judgments by a meaningful choice of concrete detail. Thus the opening passage of *The Fifth Queen* simultaneously sets the first scene and establishes an attitude of disapproval toward the party of the English Reformation:

> MAGISTER NICHOLAS UDAL, the Lady Mary's pedagogue, was very hungry and very cold. He stood undecided in the mud of a lane in the Austin Friars. The quickset hedges on either side were only waist high and did not shelter him. The little houses all round him of white daub with grey corner beams had been part of the old friars' stables and offices. All that neighbourhood was a maze of dwellings and gardens, with the hedges dry, the orchard trees bare with frost, the arbours wintry and deserted. This congregation of small cottages was like a patch of common that squatters had taken; the great house of the Lord Privy Seal, who had pulled down the monastery to make room for it, was a central mass. Its gilded vanes were in the shape of men at arms, and tore the ragged clouds with the banners on their lances.[6]

---

6. Ford Madox Hueffer, *The Fifth Queen: And How She Came to*

The transformation of the "old friars' stables and offices" into a "congregation" of Lutheran cottages "like a patch of common that squatters had taken" and the destruction of the old monastery for Cromwell's "great house" with "gilded vanes" tell us that citizens and statesmen alike have profited materially from dissolving the old dispensation. The "men at arms" that "tore the ragged clouds" with their banners advise us, further, of the violence inherent in the new alliance of national state and church, violence that culminates in the trilogy in Katharine's execution.

This narrative voice, in its detachment, its economy, its significant detail, anticipates the voice that speaks intermittently in *Parade's End.* Yet, serviceable as it is, the narrative prose of the Tudor trilogy suffers from a studied simplicity of syntax and diction. For the most part, Ford limits himself to a few syntactic forms: simple sentences, compound sentences, main clauses followed by single subordinate clauses usually introduced by "for." And he repeats again and again a small number of adjectives such as *little, great, huge, heavy, ill,* and *goodly.* Undoubtedly, Ford tries to, and does, impart an antique or archaic quality to his narrative. But the predictability of his sentences is tedious, and he overworks the device of adjectival repetition.

Unfortunately, the second style of the trilogy does not enjoy even a limited success. Ford's direct discourse is ill suited to relieve the weight of numerous lengthy dramatic scenes. It is neither brisk nor witty nor is it, finally, informative. It is essentially declamation, addressing its appeal primarily to the ear. Consider, for example, the following speech of Katharine Howard's:

> "I have listened to thee; listen thou to me. Thou art so filthy that if thou couldst make me a queen by the touch of a finger, I had rather be a goose-girl and eat grass. If by thy forged tales I could cast down Mahound, I had rather be his slave than thy accomplice! Could I lift my head if I had joined myself to thee? thou Judas to the Fiend. Junius Brutus, when he did lay siege to a town, had a citizen come to him that would play the traitor. He accepted his proffered help, and when the town was taken he did flay the betrayer. But thou art so filthy that thou shouldst

Court (London: Alston Rivers, 1906), p. 1. All subsequent references in the text will be to this edition.

make me do better than that noble Roman, for I would flay thee, disdaining to be aided by thee; and upon thy skin I would write a message to thy master saying that thou wouldst have betrayed him!" (*FQ*, pp. 196-197).

The inflated diction, the pretentious allusions, the inverted syntax, the highly artificial rhythm (most of the passage may be scanned as verse)—all make for slow and sleepy reading. Besides, Ford neglects too much of the necessary business of the novelist while he pursues poetic effect. Not only does his narrative advance at snail's pace but his characters remain undeveloped. The declamatory style obviously does not convey the quick mental action and reaction of an individual under stress. Neither does it express personal differences. Katharine Howard speaks in the same measured manner whether she hires a new maid-in-waiting or makes a false and fatal confession of adultery, and her manner is much the same as that of a number of other members of Henry VIII's court.

The narrative voice focuses again and again on physical appearances in an effort to show that the characters feel as well as speak. But their gestures and facial expressions are usually as studied as their words. Throughout the trilogy, bodies *sway, totter,* and *bend,* arms *slowly rise and fall,* heads *nod backward and forward,* jaws *drop,* eyelids *close,* complexions *blanch with fear* and *redden with anger*—all with unconvincing regularity. Despite the convictions of critics, Ford's historical personages do not "live as human beings." They are stiff-jointed marionettes, making unnatural gestures, uttering artificial speeches against a series of backdrops pieced together from antiquarian sources.

Significantly enough, Ford's lengthy excursion away from an intimate point of view and a colloquial style runs parallel to an extended evasion of subject. In the Tudor trilogy, Ford chooses to create a romantic heroine; but he just begins to come to terms with her in the last pages of *The Fifth Queen Crowned* and then he shows that he does not understand her and cannot achieve a consistent evaluation of her code of conduct.

Ford follows history by submitting his heroine to a charge of adultery—a capital crime for a queen. But he departs if not from history at least from the consensus of historical opinion by making her innocent of that charge. The Katharine Howard of the trilogy is falsely accused. She is persecuted by enemies, and enemies and sometime friends alike perjure themselves to support her false indictment. While Ford does not take his heroine through a formal trial, he does set a final dramatic scene where she stands face to face with her accusers. Katharine surprises Henry VIII and the Lords of his Council in the act of deliberating her fate and, despite her innocence, proceeds to confess to "adultery and all such sins."[7] Henry drives the Lords away and orders his wife to recant. She does not. But she does explain precisely why she has confessed to crimes she has not committed. In effect, she presents an extended defense of herself.

That defense goes unanswered in the dramatic action. *The Fifth Queen Crowned* concludes with a simple notation of Katharine's execution on Tower Hill. But by virtue of his final scene, indeed by virtue of the direction of his entire trilogy, Ford raises a moral issue. Is Katharine innocent not only of the crime of which she is accused but innocent in a larger moral sense as well? Or does she speak from a vulnerable position, so that we ourselves challenge her last words and pronounce a judgment on her?

During the first two volumes of the trilogy, Ford seems to be preparing for the second possibility. Katharine Howard arrives at Greenwich Palace unsophisticated in the Machiavellian ways of the Tudor court. She has read widely in the Latin moralists; she clings to the old Roman faith; and she becomes a self-appointed apologist for a Christian-humanistic code of conduct. Honesty, selflessness, and the courage of their convictions are the lessons she urges on the worldlings around her. In particular, she bids them bow to Rome and restore the property they have recently taken from the church. With all her preaching, however, Katharine changes very few hearts. Even her friends repeatedly question her standards of action. Men have never, they say, achieved the goodness she counsels and never will achieve it. And indeed, while she moralizes, Katharine herself falls short of her principles. Although she idealizes Henry as a king who will lead his country back to Rome, she sees him also as a giver of gifts and dreams for herself

---

7. Ford Madox Hueffer, *The Fifth Queen Crowned: A Romance* (London: Eveleigh Nash, 1908), p. 303. All subsequent references in the text will be to this edition.

a destiny in which even her faith subserves her wish for personal glory: "She itched to be Queen—on the morrow or next day; she desired to have the King for her own, to wear fair gowns and a crown; to be beloved of the poor people and beloved of the saints."[8]

Throughout *The Fifth Queen* and *Privy Seal* Katharine wavers between the two poles of her desire, between her longing for righteousness and her longing for advancement, between self-denial and self-gratification. At the end of *Privy Seal,* she adopts a compromise position. She agrees to marry the king, but begs to be excused from formal coronation because she fears she has been ambitious. Thus Katharine is not above moral reproach. In the society in which she moves she is only comparatively innocent.

With the beginning of *The Fifth Queen Crowned,* however, Ford's attitude toward his heroine undergoes a radical change. He dismisses Katharine's internal conflict, and he virtually ceases to criticize her.[9] Childish and capricious before, Katharine is now mature and steadfast—patient with others' impatience, kind in the face of their cruelty. She is no longer merely the arbiter of good conduct but the exemplar as well. In *The Fifth Queen Crowned,* indeed, Katharine's only flaw is practical rather than moral. She cannot see the malice around her; so she fails to protect herself against it. But her lack of perception is reason for praise rather than blame, because it is strictly a function of her innocence. Even her previous behavior now becomes subject to reinterpretation. In the first two novels, several passages suggest that Katharine was guilty of intimacy with her cousin Culpepper before she came to court. In the third novel, every reference to their relationship points to the contrary conclusion. Katharine thus stands in plain good-to-evil opposition to her enemies. They accuse her of adultery because she has nearly persuaded the king to make his peace with Rome, and they oppose a return to Rome because they do not want to forfeit their ecclesiastical spoils. For his part, the king believes her inno-

---

8. Ford Madox Hueffer, *Privy Seal: His Last Venture* (London: Alston Rivers, 1907), p. 197.

9. John A. Meixner notes this change in Ford's characterization of Katharine. In *The Fifth Queen Crowned,* Meixner writes, Katharine "turns into a stock sentimental heroine" (*Ford Madox Ford's Novels: A Critical Study* [Minneapolis, 1962], p. 62).

cent. But his subjects call him cuckold, and vanity prompts him to seek an annulment of his marriage.

If we could judge Katharine's final speech only by ear, if we could ignore her logic and listen only to her rhetoric, we would be convinced that her last words achieve her apotheosis as a martyr to her faith. She would become, quite simply, a romantic heroine who chooses death before dishonor. But the mind attends as well as the ear, and Katharine's utterance is rent by contradiction. It throws into doubt the entire system of values of *The Fifth Queen Crowned*, of the whole trilogy.

In part, Katharine appears to speak from a position consistent with the code of conduct she upholds throughout the trilogy. She speaks, in part, as an uncompromising idealist. When Henry tells her he has arranged, on the basis of a lie, to annul their marriage publicly and promises to submit to the Pope if she will become his mistress privately, she immediately refuses his offer. She goes on to say that she has confessed falsely and guaranteed her own execution in order to save herself from moral compromise. "For, if I had not so ensured and made [my execution] fated, I might later have wavered.[. . .] Now I am assured of death, and know that no means of yours can save me, nor no prayers nor yielding of mine" (*FQC*, p. 309).

So much for Katharine, evangelist of the old faith and humanist. For the rest, her speech develops a different ethic, an ethic very much at odds with her Christian-humanistic role. She has confessed, she says, to "adultery and all such sins" in order to punish Henry for his lack of faith in her. At the same time, she claims that she has confessed in order to punish herself. "I hope," she says, "that this sin [of falsehood] that brings me down shall counterbalance that other [of ambition] that set me up" (*FQC*, pp. 309-310). She thus assumes a power beyond any her state offers, for she passes judgment on her king, and beyond any her religion sanctions, for she deals out penance to her own soul.

In a manner appropriate to her new stance, she reviles Henry:

"You appeared to me such a man as was Pompey the Great, or as was Marius, or as was Sylla. For each of these great men erred; yet they erred greatly as rulers that would rule. Or rather I did see you such a one as was Caesar Julius, who, as you well wot, crossed a Rubicon and set out upon a high endeavour. But you—never will you cross any Rubicon; always you blow hot in the evening and cold at dawn. Neither do you, as I had dreamed you did, rule in this your realm. For, even as a crow that just now I watched, you are blown hither and thither by every gust that blows. Now the wind of gossips blows so that you must have my life" (*FQC*, pp. 307-308).

She criticizes the king for what is essentially a failure in decisiveness and passion. According to her point of view now, a man's principles are irrelevant; his moral worth depends solely on his gusto and single-mindedness. It does not matter if he errs as long as he errs "greatly."

Katharine Howard is a romantic protagonist who enters experience with an ideal code of conduct and seeks to fulfill a heroic and morally irreproachable conception of herself. For much of his trilogy, Ford is disposed to criticize his heroine, to suggest that her code is too stringent and she herself over-ambitious in trying to meet it. Then, in *The Fifth Queen Crowned*, he suddenly grants full approval to his heroine, and goes on to supply two contradictory rationales for it. He allows Katharine to vindicate herself both within and without a social framework. As a Christian and a humanist, she dies to attest the goodness of a social order superior to the one she lives in; as an apologist for reckless self-expression, she dies to deny all order. The self rejects all commitments—to the king as husband and ruler, to the state, to the church—save its commitment to its own need for self-assertion. In every sense, then, her words are last words. But they pay simultaneous tribute to inconsistent values and therefore reveal their author's intellectual and emotional confusion. We *do* pronounce a judgment, but not within the world of the trilogy, not under the guidance of its creator.

I suggest, at the risk of some simplification, that two Katharine Howards appear in the Tudor trilogy. The challenge for one is the *subjection* of individualistic impulses *to* ideal values. The challenge for the other is the *liberation* of individualistic impulses *from* ideal values. Each heroine meets the challenge successfully, and the curious last scene presents the antithetical glorification of both the Christian martyr and the immoralist.

In the trilogy, then, Ford is still unable to reconcile the inconsistent values of *The Shifting of the Fire* and *The Inheritors*. He continues to admire both self-control and self-expression; he continues to sanction a strict moral code and lawlessness. And he tends to write novels that avoid his central areas of ambivalent feeling and thought and that simplify both character and conflict. After an attempt at internal tension in the first two volumes of the Tudor trilogy, he turns to wholly external strife. As a result, Katharine Howard is not really tested by circumstances until the final pages of *The Fifth Queen Crowned,* when she learns that her idealistic code does not work in the world. Here at last Ford reaches a potentially rich dramatic situation; and here he concludes his narrative, where he might better have begun it. *The Good Soldier* discovers Dowell already on the rack of disillusion and *Parade's End* follows Christopher Tietjens through disillusion to moral regeneration. But the trilogy simply allows Katharine Howard to make an immediate and triumphant adjustment to the bitterness of truth. Whether as martyr or immoralist, Katharine enjoys the immense satisfaction of her own righteousness. The fact that her final victory is pyrrhic—for martyr and immoralist alike the end is the block on Tower Hill—only serves the better to condemn King, courtiers, menials, all the Tudor court. Katharine is very good, the rest of her world very bad.

The Tudor trilogy, it may be just as well to repeat at this point, is the work of a deliberate (though uninspired) craftsman, and it is therefore instructive in relation to the rest of Ford's historical romances. It suggests that their sentimentality may proceed from more than a desire to win commercial success. An evasion of internal tension, a facile solution to conflict—these are convenient, perhaps even inevitable shifts for the novelist who is torn by irreconcilable emotional and intellectual loyalties. The difficult task of integration, or at least of balance, is likely to be abandoned for easy exaggeration of one kind or another. The result is an unconvincing world, too black and too white to resemble the one that really turns on its axis.

Although Ford wrote four more historical novels before the first war, I propose to consider here just *The 'Half Moon'* and *The Young Lovell,* because they not only return to the situation of Katharine Howard—in effect, the second variation of Ford's "story"[10]—but

---

10. The second version of Ford's "story" appears, earlier, in

evaluate it in new ways. Perhaps more than any other of the early novels they show the extent to which Ford experimented in content before *The Good Soldier*. Both are very similar technically. In style and point of view, they essentially repeat the Tudor trilogy. But they are, fortunately, freer in syntax and diction. Fortunately also, Ford relies less heavily on dramatic scene and hence on declamation. He is more willing to telescope his action and to present it through the eyes of one or the other of his characters. Both *The 'Half Moon'* and *The Young Lovell* give the over-all impression of being less studied, less inhibited performances than the trilogy. Alike in technique, the novels are, however, very different in the disposition they make of their narrative components. And although neither qualifies as distinguished fiction, each moves away from the contradictions of *The Fifth Queen Crowned* to achieve intellectual coherence. Taken together, they point toward the moral attitudes of Ford's mature work.

In comparison with the Tudor trilogy, *The 'Half Moon'* is a surprisingly untroubled novel. It is Ford's best adventure story. It moves quickly from seventeenth-century Rye to Amsterdam to the as yet unnamed island of Manhattan, there to conclude without losing explicit thematic control.

At first glance, *The 'Half Moon'* appears to present a protagonist

---

Romance, for which Ford again supplied the plot. There the hero-narrator John Kemp sets up for himself, as an Englishman and a gentleman, a scrupulous code of honor: he risks his life protecting the innocent and defenseless, treats the girl he loves with exquisite gallantry, and twice refuses to kill unforgiving enemies rather than take unfair advantage of them. But his heroism and his chivalry give impetus to nearly disastrous consequences. He is suspected of fornication, fraud, sedition, and attempted murder. At the climax of *Romance,* he stands trial at the Old Bailey on the capital charge of piracy. He escapes the hangman at last, thanks only to chance and the conventions of popular fiction. But he does not escape moral judgment. In this collaborative novel, in which Conrad's part was considerable, the hero is forced to admit his egoism; his own thirst for glory has led him to the humiliation of the prisoner's box at the Old Bailey.

Resemblances to the Tudor trilogy are plain, as are differences. In the trilogy, Ford repeats the key elements of the plot of *Romance* but, working alone, he is unable to arrive at a stable evaluation of his romantic protagonist.

similar to Katharine Howard. Edward Colman, merchant, ship-builder, and Baron of the free port of Rye, is an "idealist" and a "searcher after the future."[11] He believes in an ethic different from that of his society, and, as a result of malice and circumstances, he suffers in exile and eventually dies. Yet, while Colman's career iterates in various ways the destiny of Katharine Howard, Colman is essentially unlike Ford's romantic heroine. He is not proud; he is not an egoist; he is not over-ambitious. In fact, the novel employs Colman to celebrate the virtues of honest industry and home. He is happily married to, and regretfully parts from, Magdalena, a good housekeeper who exemplifies the feminine equivalents of her husband's practical virtues: she cleans, sews, weaves, and keeps flawless domestic accounts. Furthermore, although Colman's ethic is different from that of his society, it is not always more strict. Colman does not wish to overturn the status quo in England; he merely wants to modify it in certain ways—to allow tolerance, for example, to various dissenting sects already established and to give up the ancient privileges of the Cinque Ports when they are no longer practicable. He is, in other words, a pragmatist, disposed to suit his ethic to circumstances. And he neither claims nor wishes for an ideal goodness but rather one that accords with life as it is.

At the same time that he frees his hero from idealism and presumption, however, Ford does incorporate the most distinctive qualities of Katharine Howard in The 'Half Moon'. He splits them between Anne Jeal, a woman Colman refuses to marry, and Henry Hudson, whose crew Colman joins. Anne is an egoist. And Anne is reckless, single-minded, and vengeful. She claims to be capable of emotion more intense than any Colman or Magdalena can experience; after Colman rejects her, she risks her life trying to bring him to execution. She is even a literal witch, melting waxen images over her fire, brewing storms by twirling peas in a sieve. For his part, Henry Hudson covets glory; he is willing to gamble the lives of himself and his crew in order to gain it.

Hudson is a foil for Colman, as Anne Jeal is for Magdalena. Indeed, Ford's strategy in The 'Half Moon' is obvious. He fashions

11. Ford Madox Hueffer, The 'Half Moon': A Romance of the Old World and the New (New York: Doubleday, Page, 1909), pp. xiii-xiv. All subsequent references in the text will be to this edition.

a new hero and heroine from materials that are "safe." He relegates his "dangerous" materials, those he cannot handle without contradiction, to Anne Jeal and Henry Hudson; and he condemns both the witch and the vain old man. Finally, he transmutes the sorrow of his hero's death into joy as Magdalena looks forward to joining her husband someday in heaven. "Of all things in the world," she peacefully remarks at the novel's end, "the strongest are patience and love" (p. 340).

Plainly *The 'Half Moon'* is a story of the fair-haired and the dark. The characters are sentimental conceptions, meeting only in external combat with one another. Colman, for example, may be harangued, exiled, and even killed. But he is proof against the temptations of vanity, glory, and reckless passion. He engages us simply as a figure in an exciting story and, once his fate is known, there is virtually no more to learn. Patience and love are very strong indeed when they are possessed in such liberal amounts.

Perhaps *The 'Half Moon'* makes concessions to commercialism. Its subject and its date of publication both suggest that it was aimed at a popular audience—it appeared, in New York as well as London, on the tercentenary anniversary of the voyage it re-creates. Nonetheless, it remains of interest, partly for its own sake as good adventure, partly for the insight it provides into Ford's development. The disposition of its narrative components suggests that Ford was, at least as early as 1909,[12] fairly conscious of the difficulties he faced in the evaluation of the "one story" he had to tell. The lines of combat are too clearly drawn, the villains too neatly placed, to admit of accidental arrangement. In comparison with the confusion and illogic of the Tudor trilogy, perhaps coherence of any kind would be welcome. The particular coherence of *The 'Half Moon'* is more than welcome: it is promising, too. Its pragmatic ethic represents a compromise between two Fordian extremes of morality and action, between, say, the fastidious propriety of Clement Hollebone and the

---

12. Although *The 'Half Moon'* was published in 1909, Ford dates his dedicatory letter June 8, 1907. He may therefore have written *The 'Half Moon'* before, or contemporaneously with, the last volume of his Tudor trilogy. He may, in other words, have dealt consistently with a "safe" hero even before, or at the same time that, he lost control of his romantic protagonist Katharine Howard.

reckless egoism of Edith Ryland, between Katharine Howard's impeccable code of conduct and her nihilism. *The 'Half Moon'*, then, suggests that Ford's ethical attitudes were changing,[13] and a glance ahead at his best work suggests that the direction of the change was destined to be a fruitful one. Love that takes things as they are is a value by implication in *The Good Soldier*. Love, patience, and hard work are values in *Parade's End*.

Still, a logical compromise between extremes and a coherent moral point of view do not alone lead to great fiction. The pragmatic ethic of *The 'Half Moon'* might be promising. But a protagonist born to temperance and a wicked witch were not. Ford had yet to return to the romantic heroes and the independent heroines who stirred his imagination far more than Colman, Magdalena, Anne Jeal, and Henry Hudson. He had to liberate vanity, glory, passion, recklessness and reconcile them with his new scheme of values.

Because it makes some progress toward such liberation and reconciliation, *The Young Lovell* is another interesting early work. Once again, Ford simplifies his issues of conflict and produces a smooth, superficial narrative. But, in this last historical romance of his apprenticeship, he achieves intellectual coherence at the same time that he creates a romantic hero. Lovell is a knight in Northumberland at the time of Henry VII. He is, in part, a public man, an exemplar of a rigorous code of social responsibility. And the feudal order he represents is threatened by the new instruments of the Tudor king, bureaucracy and commercialism. Lovell is therefore an embattled leader, almost an anachronism, protecting his castle, his lands, his vassals, from selfish interests.

---

13. The first version of *Ladies Whose Bright Eyes: A Romance*, published in 1911, repeats essentially the same ethic as *The 'Half Moon.'* *Ladies* translates a Philistine publisher from twentieth-century London to fourteenth-century Wiltshire and teaches him that "it is one's business to make a good job of what one's got in hand" (London: Constable, 1919, p. 357). In Wiltshire, William Sorrell learns to value both domestic and feudal responsibility; and, returned to London, he applies his lessons to modern times. He conceives of a sound marriage as the foundation of a new life, and he plans to publish worthwhile books rather than merely profitable ones. (In a later version of *Ladies*, published in 1935, hero and heroine aim to fulfill their ethical ideals not in England but in the Caucasus.)

Lovell is also, in part, an individual who has experienced a vision of private, and anti-social, happiness. On the morning he is to enter formally into his chivalric inheritance, he rides out from his chapel and sees a fair lady seated on a white horse. She appears to beckon him; she bewitches him. As he stands and watches her, three months pass as a day. When he returns to his castle, he suffers the usual fate of the hero in the second version of Ford's "story." He finds that he has been accused of a crime, sorcery, and that his enemies have sworn false evidence against him. He has lost his reputation; his social position has been usurped by a wicked half-brother. Decies has seized Lovell's title and inheritance and allowed the traditional ties of feudalism to lapse.

Lovell proceeds to set his affairs in order, arrogantly, contemptuously, with all the defiant self-righteousness displayed by Katharine Howard before Henry and his lords. At the same time, he feels "a sudden weariness, like the sound of a story heard over and over again."[14] His chivalric duties are joyless, and he longs for the happiness the beckoning lady appeared to promise. The lady is identified precisely by a wise old bishop as "the spirit that most snareth men to carnal desires" (p. 238). The narrative thus becomes an allegory of struggle between conscience and senses. The hero's conflict is therefore paradoxical. As a knight, he fights enemies who dissipate his inheritance on good food, choice wine, and women. As a man bewitched, he is tempted himself to yield to sensuality.

Eventually, Lovell satisfies the demands of conscience. He reorganizes his vassals according to feudal order, ousts his usurper, regains his castle. He publicly plays, in other words, the responsible role to which he is born. Then, just as his castle is won, he disappears. He pays in secret the spiritual price of his sensual love. Unworthy of the chivalric code by which he has outwardly acted, he does penance by turning hermit, by entering for the rest of his life an anchorite's dwelling.

To this point, the novel acquiesces in Lovell's judgment of himself and seems to say that, while men create strict standards of morality, even the best of men must fail to meet those standards.

14. Ford Madox Hueffer, *The Young Lovell: A Romance* (London: Chatto & Windus, 1913), p. 218. All subsequent references to this novel will appear in the text.

Even the best are guilty rather than innocent, although they are not necessarily guilty of the crimes of which society accuses them. Their furthest limit of virtue is therefore self-destruction. Failing to assert the demands of conscience over the demands of the senses, they can at least, by one last effort of will, deliver themselves entirely from the scene of temptation.

Yet *The Young Lovell* is only part historical romance. In its last pages Ford presents another, and fantastical, realm of experience. He transfers his scene to a valley high in Corsica where a feminine deity occupies a marble throne in fields of asphodels. Among her lieges, is the young Lovell, who thinks no more on the "weariness of Northumberland" or on his "mortal body" confined in its narrow religious cell:

> No, there they lay or walked in lemon groves devising of this or that whilst the butterflies settled upon their arms. And when they would have it night, so there was the cool of the evening and a great moon and huge stars and dimness fit for the gentle pleasures of love (p. 310).

This conclusion, of course, changes the significance of the novel, for the valley of Corsica functions as an ironic criticism of Lovell's self-abnegation. His anchoritic existence at home is paralleled by a richly sensual life abroad, or, to transpose the allegory into psychological terms, the emotions he tries to suppress by his retirement from the real world find expression in an imaginative world of daydreams. Lovell, too, is an egoist who reaches for an over-ambitious ideal of virtue.

The Young Lovell, then, does not repeat the pragmatic ethic of *The 'Half Moon'*. Yet, significantly, neither does it contradict that ethic. For the first time, Ford succeeds in controlling his moral attitude toward a romantic protagonist. He deals with his own "dangerous" materials and reduces them to firm intellectual coherence. The final irony of *The Young Lovell* may reasonably be regarded as a development toward a novel that would present a romantic hero and yet relinquish romantic ideals. If the hero's conscience leads to self-destruction, and he allows his senses to find fulfillment only in a never-never land, then this world offers him no happiness whatsoever—unless he changes his original code of conduct, as well as his image of himself, and comes to terms with reality.

The Young Lovell, as I have already noted, suffers from the same simplification of character as *The 'Half Moon'*, although it would be more accurate to say that the characters are not so much superficial as they are remote. The novel concentrates on Lovell's external struggle and concentrates, particularly and often to the point of tedium, on the background of that struggle, on details of feudal fortifications, weapons, and administration. In contrast with these extended passages of medievalism, the brief and occasional dream-like moments of Lovell's reflections on the beckoning lady are very well done. The hero's longing, his distraction from the military task at hand are convincingly presented. The life of the novel clearly dwells just off-stage, in a personal relationship that receives relatively little attention.

In his historical romances, Ford did succeed in resolving his ambivalent moral and emotional attitudes toward his material. But when he turned from England's present to her past, he resorted also to easy and superficial terms of conflict. He had, still, to come to terms with his own times. And, still, to create protagonists who would compel our belief and more than our momentary curiosity. In certain of the modern novels he wrote between *The Inheritors* and *The Good Soldier*, he was trying with considerable difficulty to find the realistic equivalents of witches and mistresses of faerie, of a compensating heaven and fields of asphodels; he was attempting the psychological complexity he so clearly evaded in the Tudor trilogy, *The 'Half Moon,'* and *The Young Lovell*.

CHAPTER 3

Better Ones

IN COMPARISON with his historical romances, Ford's love stories and satires of contemporary life are markedly uneven in quality. They contain some of the best and some of the worst passages he wrote before the first war. Along with many clear prefigurations, in character and scene, even in patterns of imagery, of *The Good Soldier* and *Parade's End,* they possess, often in liberal amounts, the wit and humor so noticeably absent from most of the historical romances.[1] But they also present a high proportion of irrelevant narrative, of diffuse debate. Many of them tend to culminate, one way or another, in insignificance; to arrive at a thematic impasse; or else to end with a general expository statement that is simply added to, rather than derived from, the action. All of them aim at a criticism of modern English values and institutions, though they do not all achieve it.

Ford does not hesitate to use fantasy and bring the impossible into conjunction with the real even in his re-creations of contemporary life. *Mr. Apollo* precipitates the god of the title into London in order to expose the personal aims of the "servants" of society—the ministry, the press, the radical intelligentsia. *The New Humpty-Dumpty* creates an unlikely kingdom to score English divorce law and, again, radical intellectuals. *Mr. Fleight* (1913)

---

1. *The Portrait* has a fair share of wit, as does *Ladies Whose Bright Eyes.* Kenneth Young (*Ford Madox Ford,* p. 25) finds a "most delicious gift of the comic" in the Tudor trilogy, but Ford's attempts at humor there are, in fact, heavy-handed.

exaggerates the corruption of English party politics beyond the limits of fact. All these increasingly somber fantasy-satires, as well as the lighter *Simple Life Limited* and *Panel,* which are directed in part against literary figures and practices, provide some insight into Ford's long apprenticeship. In retrospect, however, three modern love stories seem to warrant more critical attention.[2] More than the satires, *The Benefactor, An English Girl,* and *A Call* repeatedly attempt to solve crucial problems of characterization and theme. All return to the hesitant hero and independent heroine of *The Inheritors,* and they try to define in increasing detail the relationship of these characters to each other and to the traditional English moral code. They work, albeit with great uncertainty, toward the subtle psychological realism and the ethical point of view of *The Good Soldier* and *Parade's End;* they may justly be called novels of discovery.

Like an old piece of silver plate, *The Benefactor* shines—but only in places. At times, particularly in the opening chapters, Ford speaks in a coy narrative voice reminiscent of that of *The Shifting of the Fire.* At times he composes extended passages in the manner of Henry James. On at least one occasion he chooses to remember Conrad and refers to "ironical and inscrutable destiny."[3] And he writes like his own better self, the diction and rhythms colloquial, the syntax simple, the statement straight to the point. The result of so much variety, obviously, is a disjointed performance. There are abrupt and disconcerting shifts in tone, in distance, in pace. Sometimes, there are shifts in character and in the nature of personal relationships. The heroine, for example, may speak to the hero in a typically candid Fordian mode, then, just a few pages later, exchange stiff and artificial "remarks" with him in weak

---

2. The generic distinction here is not a hard and fast one. The satires all deal with love, and the love stories are also satiric. But the love stories focus principally upon the relationship between hero and heroine, while the satires treat it as a subsidiary interest. Since I shall discuss at length Ford's characterization in *The Benefactor, An English Girl,* and *A Call,* I shall of necessity give even more emphasis to love, as opposed to social satire, than the novels themselves do.

3. Ford Madox Hueffer, *The Benefactor: A Tale of a Small Circle* (London: Brown, Langham, 1905), p. 341. All subsequent references to this novel will appear in the text.

imitation of James. All these instabilities, of style, of character—and some of narrative focus as well—suggest that Ford is groping for his subject, circling its periphery but unable to find its true center.

Like *The Shifting of the Fire* and *The Inheritors, The Benefactor* dramatizes the conflict between social responsibility and self-expression in terms of a man and a woman in love. George Moffat, the hero whom the title describes, is a middle-aged poet who neglects his art to play the patron to other men of talent. As the action unfolds, it becomes clear that Moffat's generosity is at least impractical—it brings him finally to the point of bankruptcy—and may be worse. For Moffat encourages any man of artistic promise, regardless of character. Because he refuses to draw moral distinctions, he becomes the protector of the unscrupulous and the socially undesirable. One of his protégés involves his sister-in-law in a questionable scheme to "push" Spanish art. Another protégé marries Dora Brede, the heroine's younger sister, and treats her viciously. Though Moffat himself is married, his wife has long since left him because her religious principles will not allow her to tolerate her husband's indifference to moral character. Finally, Moffat discovers that in attempting to help her family, he has fallen in love with the heroine, Clara Brede, whom he cannot marry.

Unlike Moffat, Clara has never enjoyed leisure or freedom. In the past, she has nursed her mother. Now she nurses her father. Mr. Brede is convinced that he has killed his wife and his guilt has caused him to suffer a nervous breakdown. So Clara must cope with her father's excesses of remorse, with his intermittent threats to cut his throat. She meets her responsibilities, as she always has. But by the time she falls in love with Moffat, she has begun to resent the demands of family duties. Indeed, she doubts even the wisdom of self-denial.

Except when she participates in Jamesian conversations, Clara is a vigorously drawn portrait and Ford is at his best in *The Benefactor* when he deals with her. She is clearly a prefiguration of Valentine Wannop, in *Parade's End*, in her rather plain and sturdy appearance, in her straightforward manner, and even, in a general way, in her family history. (Mr. Brede is incapable of pursuing his profession as a clergyman. Mr. Wannop dies, leaving his family destitute. In both cases, the daughters are compelled to keep the homes of parents, and in both cases they are rebellious.)

Clara admits her dissatisfaction with her life to Moffat who, in turn, admits his own dissatisfaction. He has begun to regret the indirection of his life and also to realize the unfortunate consequences of his indiscriminate benevolence. To Clara, he sums up their respective situations: "We've precisely the opposite desires. [. . .] I feel myself so miserably wanting in the purposefulness you want to get rid of" (p. 192). At the conclusion of the novel, a succession of catastrophes forces each of them to a decision. Since they cannot marry, they must decide whether they will or will not live together abroad, whether they will live without or within the conventional code of morality. True to pre-established form, they come to opposite conclusions. Clara is ready for Italy; but Moffat, after much decision and revision and even after a proposal voiced with almost Jamesian delicacy, is not. *The Benefactor* follows, to borrow a phrase from E. M. Forster, an hourglass pattern. At the end of the narrative the hero and heroine have changed places. Clara has sloughed her initial burden of social responsibility, and Moffat has taken it up. *The Benefactor* endorses neither position, and its conclusion is unsatisfactory—because of the peculiar nature of its indecision.

Ford works hard and melodramatically to clear the ground for Moffat's last choice; he levels all practical impediments to life with Clara. A novel, tossed off years ago and now belatedly published, brings Moffat a new fortune. Marriage has already removed her younger sister from Clara's household. Now a lapse into incurable insanity removes her father. Mr. Brede goes mad in the midst of preaching a sermon; he tears his pulpit apart, then withdraws into a state in which he neither hears nor speaks. Moffat drives him to an insane asylum. Clearly only his own reluctance to commit adultery, to break so decisively and so flagrantly the conventional moral code, finally separates Moffat from Clara.

Even this scruple temporarily yields to further reflection. Moffat for a while believes that his responsibility to Clara outweighs his recently awakened sense of social responsibility. Clara has been left alone. His primary allegiance is not to society but to her, and it is an allegiance, of course, that seems to coincide with his own desires. He tactfully makes his offer of life together abroad.

It is in the final scene of the novel that he changes his mind. His offer is scarcely made and accepted when he withdraws it, for reasons that remain, in part, obscure. With his mind's eye he sees Mr. Brede, huddled silently, massively, in the corner of a carriage, en route to the asylum:

> [Moffat] seemed to hear men's voices say, "Oh, Brede. He's in a lunatic asylum, and his daughter ran away with a married man." That contempt would fall on the memory of this man that they had both loved [. . .] it would be a final and despicable treachery (p. 346).

To this point, Moffat may appear to exercise the social conscience he has acquired in the course of the novel. "One doesn't," as he has thought in a previous moment of realization, "take a woman to the back of beyond" (p. 279). One doesn't, even more certainly, take the daughter of one's friend, even if that friend is hopelessly mad. The traditional English code of morality forbids that "final and despicable treachery."

But Moffat's train of thought continues:

> The horror of that long drive in the dark became appalling in his memory. He had been calm then, like a person stupefied. Now he saw it as something black and evil, a retribution for the ignoble course of events that had swept every obstacle away. It had given him her love, it had forced upon him the money that should make possible their life together, it had swept aside her father. But that memory and that past had risen up, a thing more dreadful than any disaster in the future (p. 347).

In effect, Moffat ceases to reason; in withdrawing his offer from Clara, he finally acts in response to a dread he does not understand but cannot dismiss. His motivation presents several difficulties. In the first place, the trip to the asylum is scarcely an appropriate symbol of remorse for Moffat. He is not responsible for Mr. Brede's madness. Besides, the trip comes to symbolize much more than Moffat's remorse for any of his actions, no matter what their moral quality. It becomes "something black and evil," a punishment for the "course of events," for Clara's love and a financial windfall as well as for a contemplated breach of propriety. The trip to the asylum along with the events becomes "a thing more dreadful than any disaster in the future." Moffat is crippled by irrational feelings of guilt and fear.

The final scene, then, approaches surprising and unknown areas in Moffat's character. But Ford does not develop those areas. As the abstractions above show, he can barely articulate Moffat's feelings. He offers no more than a vaguely defined subjective state that has no adequate objective cause. Moffat's egocentricity, his detachment from "human strivings" (p. 214), and, at the very end of the novel, his pattern of remembrance and reaction—Mrs. Brede's heart attack, Mr. Brede's guilt, and Moffat's own overwhelming guilt and fear— adumbrate Dowell in *The Good Soldier*. But in *The Benefactor* Ford is still in the process of discovering his later material. He does not yet understand his hesitant hero.

Of Clara, less is said in the final scene; but she, too, appears in a new light. Previously, she has been a plain and unassuming girl, chafing at family duties but fulfilling them all the same. She has longed to "live" but has never quite had the courage. Now, however, she is ready for happiness with Moffat. In terms of her resemblances to later Ford heroines, she suddenly becomes a prototype not of Valentine Wannop in *Parade's End* but of Leonora Ashburnham in *The Good Soldier*. At Moffat's final change of mind, unfamiliar emotions rise and dominate her, emotions of "cold anger" and "cruel pride" (p. 348). Clara's transformation, certainly, is not so startling as Moffat's and, in part at least, it has credible cause. Yet, too late, the last scene reveals, in her as well, possibilities that are new and that remain unexplored.

It is possible to view the novel as a conflict in wills. Clara has the energy first to fulfill all the duties society imposes on her and then to brush them aside, while Moffat fails to commit himself to any positive action. On this psychological level, the novel approaches coherence, even though its characters are insufficiently developed. Yet to view *The Benefactor* merely as a conflict in wills is to ignore the categories the novel itself supplies for judgment. Moffat and Clara plainly embody two attitudes toward social responsibility, attitudes they appear to exchange in the course of the novel. Working with more caution than in the Tudor trilogy, Ford makes no attempt to decide between the contradictory values of self-sacrifice and self-expression, between social responsibility and lawlessness. He explains both moral positions and brings them into balance only to abandon his own prearranged categories of judgment. Moffat's newly awakened conscience does not, after all, determine his decision to give up Clara. The moral issues of the novel are swept away by the rising tide of the hero's emotions.

The Benefactor, in other words, presents its conflict in both moral and psychological terms. But it finally abandons the moral terms and relies solely on the psychological, and these undergo a radical transformation. The hero and heroine do indeed change places, but their change lacks moral significance and they themselves are so different that they appear to be virtually new characters. The same division between the apparent designs of Ford the moralist and the realizations of Ford the psychologist appears in both *An English Girl* and *A Call*.

Reflecting the influence of James not only in style but in subject, *An English Girl* transports a disaffected American hero three times across the Atlantic and induces him finally to choose between lifelong leisure in Canterbury and involvement in rough-and-ready business in New York. Ignoring, however, the Jamesian injunction to "dramatise," Ford writes much of his novel simply as discussion or essay, loosely linked by a series of episodes. At times, indeed, the major characters appear to be nothing short of England and America—and they, of course, make unwieldy protagonists. Of the three love stories I have chosen to speak of here, *An English Girl* is surely the least accomplished, and in its subtitle (*A Romance*) it may carry the mark of Ford's own disparagement. Yet, despite its very obvious shortcomings, it does, at least at intervals, explore further than its predecessors the personality of the hesitant Fordian hero.

On one level, like *The Inheritors* and *The Benefactors*, *An English Girl* pursues the theme of social responsibility. The hero, Don Collar Kelleg, is on the point of marrying Eleanor Greville, of living ever after in the genteel and cultured shade of Canterbury Cathedral when a cable tells him that his father is dead. This news from over the ocean abruptly changes Don from suitor, desultory artist, and European traveler to "the richest citizen in the world."[4] He has

---

4. Ford Madox Hueffer, *An English Girl: A Romance* (London:

inherited from his father a vast, complicated, and ill-gotten organization of trusts. And because he has a conscience, Don interrupts his plans for perpetual retirement in Canterbury. He decides to redress the wrongs of his father: he plans to break the Kelleg trusts and to spend his money for everyone's good.

He has scarcely arrived in America, however, when his illusions about his power to change the world are stripped away by businessmen whose ethics are unsavory and by citizens who balk at social and cultural reform. He further discovers that his idealistic plans are impeded by the very terms of his father's will. Although Charles Kelleg has left his fortune to his son, he has forbidden Don to alter the organization of the Kelleg interests. In complete discouragement, Don leaves his inheritance in the hands of his lawyer and returns to England to marry Eleanor. But before the wedding, he undergoes, like Moffat, a final change of mind. He decides to return again to America and the responsibilities of his fortune. Eleanor, as he knew she would, refuses to follow him.

As a story of social responsibility, *An English Girl* seems to follow its idealistic hero from isolation through illusions of grandeur to a recognition of his own limitations and those of the world to which he is heir. And the novel creates a set of values that works to endorse the hero's final decision. Disdain for public life is satirized, and so is Charles Kelleg's ebullient but immoral career of acquisition. Don chooses to enter public life and, unlike his father, he enters it with a sense of honesty and justice. But Ford's attitude toward his hero is not one of simple or even consistent admiration.

On a second level, *An English Girl* makes an uncertain but nonetheless interesting attempt at psychological exploration. Don has grown up in the Gargantuan shadow of Charles Kelleg, a swindler who devised fantastic schemes, a husband who kept an Italian mistress, a father who delighted in baiting his fastidious son. Don's attraction to Europe has been motivated in part merely by a desire to avoid his father. That he has never succeeded in asserting himself against his father's forceful personality is a psychological fact that emerges on his first return to America:

Methuen, 1907), p. 1. All subsequent references to this novel will appear in the text.

The high panels with their tapestried shepherds, the chairs with their lyre-shaped backs against the walls, the lights in clusters upon the imitation wax of the candlesticks—all these things affected him deeply with a sense of solitude, a sense of small-ness, a sense of impotence that he hadn't felt since he had been a small child. And the repeated mention of his father's name had brought a tense sense of his father again before him. His father had sat on those very chairs, had looked at those very pictures with his twinkling badger grey eyes of a man used to baffle and outwit (p. 279).

Thus *An English Girl* is not only a story of an idealist who attempts to cope with an evil inheritance but also of a son who tries to match the power of his father.

The hero confronts, as it were, the ghost of his father. He also confronts the living heroine. Both relationships are tests of maturity and, until his second return to America, he fails them both. But the novel exhibits very different attitudes toward his respective failures. Ford is invariably sympathetic when he writes of Don's memories of his father, of his consequent feelings of "smallness," "solitude," "im-potence." But he is critical, at times even contemptuous, of Don's equally immature responses to Eleanor. Don is not an ardent suitor. And in no uncertain terms, Ford repeatedly calls attention to his hero's lack of masculinity. Once, for example, Don kisses Eleanor "on the forehead" and whispers that he thinks of her "as a Papist thinks of his saints" (p. 189). On another occasion when Don is alone with Eleanor, he fails even to be affectionate. For the moment, Eleanor herself forgives him, but the language of her reflections shows Ford's contempt for his hero: "She made for him the quick excuse that he was, poor dear, after all his runnings about in foul air and squalid surroundings, in a state of nervous, quivering ex-haustion" (p. 272).

An English Girl offers no consistent interpretation of its final event. According to the social values of the novel, Don's second return to America is courageous and right. In the light of his fear of his father, also, Don's return is admirable. He is going back to face "repeated mention of his father's name" and scenes that vividly invoke his father's memory. But at the same time that Don accepts social responsibility and appears to meet at least one challenge of maturity, he escapes from Eleanor. Because of his relationship to Eleanor, his return to America appears to be the flight of a fearful bridegroom before the approaching date of his marriage. Don's journey home is at once courageous and cowardly, mature and immature.

The impasse in judgment is much the same as that in *The Benefactor*. In *An English Girl*, Ford the moralist appears to endorse social responsibility. But Ford the psychologist suggests that his hero satisfies his duty to society only by evading a duty more personal and perhaps equally cogent. For the second time, or rather for the third time if *The Inheritors* is recalled, Ford creates a final scene in which his hero and heroine say farewell. But he still cannot arrive at a firm or consistent evaluation of his unhappy love story.

To call *An English Girl* a novel of discovery, in plain view of Ford's continued confusion, may seem over-optimistic. Yet, in retrospect, Ford's treatment of Don Collar Kelleg is promising. Sexual diffidence is implicit in Etchingham Granger's actions during the Parisian episode of *The Inheritors*. Sexual diffidence, and immaturity as well, are implicit in Moffat's guilt and fear at the end of *The Benefactor*—or, more precisely, sexual diffidence and immaturity provide Moffat with the adequate motives so clearly missing from his final scene with Clara. In *An English Girl*, then, Ford succeeds in exploring Don Collar Kelleg further than his earlier heroes of the same type. Don's feelings of "solitude," of "smallness," of "impotence" will all appear, albeit in different contexts, in Dowell's behavior in *The Good Soldier*.

In retrospect again, the terms of conflict in the novel are also promising. Ford virtually makes Eleanor Greville morally unexceptionable. Although she appears first as a representative of a leisure class that seeks only its own pleasure, in the course of the novel she cuts her ties with her background and becomes simply a woman who wishes to marry the man she loves. The ultimate limit of her patience, even, is reasonable. She tolerates everything in Don save what she rightly takes to be his continued indecisiveness and diffidence. Through Eleanor, then, Ford shows a disposition not only to criticize his hero but to criticize him for reasons very different from the Conradian reasons supplied in the prevailing moral scheme of *The Inheritors*. A rigorous code of social responsibility might be morally good and adherence to it might be honorable. But, by a further convolution of thought, such a code might be subsumed by a superior standard of action. And a hero who met his responsibilities to society might, at the same time, fail to meet more compelling responsibilities. Such a hero might even use his rigorous code as a refuge from more compelling, and more difficult, responsibilities. Despite his claims to "virtue," then, he would become not honorable but morally vulnerable, not innocent but guilty. These ideas, however, are just intimated in *An English Girl*. Ford had one more early novel of love and marriage to write before he would fully realize them.

A Call is rich in possibilities of interpretation. It is, to begin with, a satire of the fashionable world of Mayfair, an exposé of vacuous lives played out in elegant drawing rooms, exclusive shops, and the promenades of Kensington Park. But if vacuity is the only achievement of this world, it is not, initially, the only possibility and *A Call* is also, like so many of Ford's other early novels, a study of the conflict between the demands of society and those of the individual. Finally, and in direct relationship to the tension between tradition and self-expression, *A Call* creates an interrelated series of psychological revelations. Each of its four main characters experiences a moment of self-realization. He becomes aware that he hides within himself emotions that Mayfair will not countenance; he finds that he himself is capable of breaking London's moral laws.

As the foregoing summary suggests, *A Call* presents its material with more audacity than either *The Benefactor* or *An English Girl*. Indeed, it introduces its hero in a stage of luckless development much later than George Moffat's and Don Collar Kelleg's. Robert Grimshaw has already refused to marry a woman he loves, and he has, besides, arranged a marriage between that woman and his best friend. The novel proceeds to unfold the causes and consequences of his actions.

In the first scene, the formal wedding of Pauline Lucas and Dudley Leicester, Grimshaw deliberately plays the role of Pauline's rejected suitor. Afterwards, he reveals another self. He does love Pauline. But he has rejected her, since he also cares for Katya Lascarides. "I suppose what I really want," he admits to a friend, "is both Katya and Pauline." Then he adds, "I've got to sacrifice physical possession of one of them to the amenities of a civilization that's pleasant enough, and that's taken thousands of years to bring together."[5] So he has married Pauline to Dudley Leicester, reserving himself for Katya. For Katya, because he was once engaged to her and as an English gentleman he still considers the agreement binding. If not optimistic about his future, Grimshaw is at least confident that he can meet the demands of "civilization" and meet them with serenity. The chances for surprise are, of course, numerous. Grimshaw has neatly disposed the private lives of Pauline, of Dudley, and of Katya. Any one of the three may jump the traces in which he drives them—or he may jump himself.

Foreshadowing all these possibilities, the novel turns to Dudley Leicester. Dudley is introduced as a comic figure—very tall, ungainly, docile. He is subject to "panics" (p. 49) about his health and his unconventional impulses. He may wish "to balance, for instance, a full glass on the top of his head, or to flip drops of wine at his neighbour's bare shoulders" (p. 51). He feels "safe" (p. 51) only as long as his wife Pauline has her eyes on him. As the novel shifts its focus to him, however, it takes him out in London—alone. Without his wife, he has one of his panics and goes mad.

Before he met Pauline, Dudley had courted Etta Stackpole,[6]

---

5. Ford Madox Hueffer, *A Call: The Tale of Two Passions* (London: Chatto & Windus, 1910), p. 34. *A Call* was also published as a serial in the *English Review*, in Volume III (August-November, 1909). Apart from numerous changes in punctuation, the book contains only occasional revisions of, and additions to, the serial. All subsequent references in the text will be to the 1910 edition.

6. The name recalls, of course, Henrietta Stackpole in *The Portrait of a Lady*. Ford's character, in her complete forthrightness and her unabashed capacity for sensual life, is an English exaggeration of James's unconventional American traveler and, very likely, a mockery of Jamesian delicacy. In *A Call*, Ford also rings a minor change on the Jamesian name Madame de Mauves, again with satiric intent: Madame de Mauvesine is a minor character who raises her eyes piously to the ceiling at Etta's antics, raises them only to encounter "a limpid blue sky filled with chains of roses and gambolling cherubs" (p. 60).

These good-natured thrusts at James (there are others in *The Panel*) concur, interestingly enough, with Ford's abandonment of serious Jamesian pastiche. *A Call* shows that he has outgrown his close stylistic dependence on James, though there are, to be sure, echoes of Jamesian since become Lady Hudson, but he had broken with her because she flirted with other men, even with Bugle the farrier's son and with Moddle the third footman. Dudley did not doubt Etta's virtue, but he feared gossip. Now, chance seats him next to Etta at a party. When his own courtesy compels him to see her home afterwards, he does it awkwardly, afraid of her and afraid of being seen with her. Then he relaxes gradually; he resolves to send Etta jonquils the next day. When they reach her door, she taunts him about his old attachment to her and suddenly pulls him into the darkness inside. Immediately, the telephone rings. Dudley picks it up. "Hitherto he had had no feeling of crime." He pretends to be Moddle the footman—but the caller asks, "Isn't that Dudley Leicester speaking?" Dudley answers honestly, "Yes," and hangs up (pp. 76-77). The admission initiates his self-revelation. He had broken with Etta because she was a flirt. Now he suddenly finds himself in a compromising position with her. That discovery, and the guilt attendant on it, quickly become so insupportable that he goes mad. His insanity takes the form of alternate violence and quiescence. Every now and then he flings himself on a stranger and demands, "Are you the fellow that rang up Mayfair 4259?" The rest of the time he remains withdrawn, completely silent.

Katya Lascarides does not, strictly speaking, experience a moment of *self*-revelation. But she does, or rather she had, some six years before the fictive present of the novel, come face-to-face with a breach in the moral code that traditionally governs relationships between men and women. When her parents died, Katya learned that they had never married. Her reaction was in its own way as intense as Dudley's response to the call in Etta Hudson's hallway. She broke her formal engagement to Grimshaw and challenged him to live with her as her father had lived with her mother. When he refused, Katya suffered a nervous breakdown.

Entering the present action of the novel, Katya meets Grimshaw in a dramatic scene of reunion. For the first time, she explains her past behavior. She recalls that her immediate response to the revelation about her parents had been shock and revulsion. She had felt a

---

prose in his best work. The line: "[Valentine] was alone with Tietjens and the quiet day," in *Some Do Not . . .* , for example, plainly borrows from the last sentence of *The Turn of the Screw*.

"loathing for all men"; she had felt a "recoiling" even from Grim-shaw (p. 119). She struggled, then, with a conflict in loyalties. If she held with convention, she had to admit that her parents were morally culpable. If she refused to judge them so, she had to break with society's traditional rules. She chose the second alternative because she came to understand, and finally to approve, her parents' conduct. They regarded formalities, she says, "as desecration" (p. 122)—wanting to rely solely on their faith in one another. Katya has long since ceased to "recoil" from Grimshaw.

Grimshaw and Pauline Leicester move toward their moments of self-revelation over a period of time until, at the end of the novel, they face their knowledge with finality and act on it. It is Pauline who frankly puts it to Grimshaw that his original plan for keeping strictly to his code of honor has failed: he still loves her, and she has been unable to keep herself from caring more and more for him. Since neither of them is proof against temptation, she counsels practical means to stay their drift toward each other. Follow, she says, Katya's advice; find the man who rang up Mayfair 4259. Then Dudley will recover and, as Grimshaw says, "we all fly as far apart as the poles" (p. 273).

During this conversation, Grimshaw recalls the crucial night when Dudley took Etta Hudson home. Unseen himself, he had seen Dudley and Etta on Regent Street. The sight forced him to admit that Dudley's marriage to Pauline—the marriage of convenience he had arranged—was a failure and that his own love for Pauline had been reasserting itself with growing intensity. The instinctive demands of human nature, he discovered, were stronger and more urgent than any respect for "civilization" or the "amenities." His code of honor was "facile"; it was "adapted only to the life of no strain" (p. 281). Under this series of shocks, Grimshaw rang up Etta Hudson's number and said, "Isn't that Dudley Leicester speaking?"

Now, in the present scene, Grimshaw publicly owns his various mistakes by confessing, first to Pauline, then to Katya, that he is the man who made the call. Then, in complete weariness, he sur-renders to Katya's terms. Katya, however, withdraws her original challenge, because of Grimshaw's attachment to Pauline. "As a precaution," she says, Grimshaw "had better" marry her after all

(p. 291). The novel ends with Katya bent over Dudley Leicester, ready to prompt him to ask, "Are you the fellow that rang up May-fair 4259?" Grimshaw is ready to answer "Yes."

When *A Call* was first published in the *English Review*, Ford was disturbed because, as he thought, various readers misinterpreted it. He therefore added an "Epistolary Epilogue" to the 1910 hard-cover edition. In that epilogue, he scores English readers for insensitivity and he also explains his novel. Its commitment to judgment, he says essentially, is "plain as a pikestaff" (p. 302). He goes on to claim, summarily, that Grimshaw was "an amiable but meddlesome and inwardly conceited fool" (p. 301), that he was "extremely in love with Pauline Leicester, and that, in the first place, by marrying her to Dudley Leicester, and, in the second place, by succumbing to a disagreeable personality, he was committing the final folly of this particular affair" (p. 302).

Ford's interpretation certainly receives some support from his novel. It is, in fact, possible to go further than Ford and find a coherent criticism not only of Grimshaw but of the other principal characters as well. According to the English code of manners, none of them is good enough. As their successive moments of self-discovery reveal, they all find themselves in conflict with the demands of "civilization." Yet these failures, while the novel does not excuse them, are merely derivative. They all proceed from one common failure: a refusal to acknowledge love and its claims. Grimshaw gives up Pauline for the sake of honor; Dudley Leicester breaks with Etta Hudson because of propriety; Pauline marries simply for convenience; and Katya resolves to possess a man who loves her less than he loves another woman. And Ford extends his criticism beyond his characters to the society they represent.

Indeed, the novel follows a clear pattern of thesis-antithesis-synthesis in its examination of convention. First Grimshaw speaks in favor of society's rules. Then Katya offers in opposition a purely personal ethic. Finally, a nameless Greek priest, during a chance meeting and debate with Grimshaw, offers a reconciliation of the two extremes of tradition and self-expression. Be brave enough, he says, to risk the instinctive counsel of emotion and then be brave enough again to face whatever punishment society doles out in consequence. And he suggests that there may be a standard of moral judgment superior to that of convention. "God," he concludes, "may well pardon" (p. 217) the deeds society condemns.

A Call, then, marks a decisive stage in the evolution of Ford's moral attitude toward his contemporary material. With this novel, he moves beyond the impasses of *The Benefactor* and *An English Girl* and resolves the contradictions of *The Shifting of the Fire* and *The Inheritors*. He explicitly rejects a rigorous social morality, in this case the traditional English code of manners, and, on an intellectual level at least, consistently substitutes for it a private morality. Thus Grimshaw and Dudley Leicester err when they place the dictates of convention above those of love. The individual has a right, even a duty, to recognize and express his own nature, his "instincts" and "emotions." Yet—and here *A Call* differs significantly from Ford's previous and intermittent allegiance to a private code—that right and that duty are not limitless. The private morality, in its furthest extension, constitutes a new social morality because the claims of one individual end where those of another begin. Pauline has no right to impose herself on a man she does not love; and Katya has no right to force Grimshaw into any union, whether lawful or lawless, because there she trespasses on *his* right as an individual.

Ford would return to this transcendence of tradition during the most fruitful part of his career as a novelist. Any thematic summary of *The Good Soldier* or of *Parade's End*, although it would differ in emphasis, would in no way contradict the moral values set forth in *A Call*. The novel has, to reiterate, the merit of intellectual coherence. Yet, this virtue granted, qualifications must at once be made. The novel's total attitude includes, of course, much more than its intellectual commitments. And the fact is that by 1909 Ford was not yet able to lend full conviction to his consistent moral point of view. The dialectic on convention, in short, runs through the least successful passages of the novel.

To begin with, Grimshaw is for the most part an implausible character. He comes to life occasionally as an indulgent listener to Katya or a sympathetic viewer of Pauline's sufferings with Dudley. But in the scenes where he himself is the focus of attention—and these are scenes crucial to the movement of the dialectic—he dwindles to a thematic contrivance. Ford's efforts to realize Grimshaw's remorse over the Leicester wedding, for example, issue in gauche and melodramatic physical description: "For the first time in his life Robert Grimshaw gazed out unseeing over his niece's head. He brushed her to one side and began to walk feverishly down the room, his white teeth gleaming with an air of fierceness through the bluish-black of his beard and moustache" (p. 27). Further, the series of facile abstractions that Ford typically sows in Grimshaw's conversation and reflection make him no more convincing. "I've got to sacrifice," Grimshaw says in reference to Pauline and Katya, "physical possession of one of them to the amenities of a civilization that's pleasant enough and that's taken thousands of years to bring together." In the face of this "sentiment," it is hard to believe that Grimshaw is really torn between the two women or that his sacrifice of Pauline is, indeed, a sacrifice. No wonder that Ford later felt obliged to state that Grimshaw was "extremely in love with Pauline Leicester"—for his characterization of his hero often fell short of his intention.

A similar failure occurs in Ford's treatment of Katya, and it occurs especially in the passages where he completes the second phase of his dialectic. Katya's own explanation of her unorthodox challenge we have already seen—she urges Grimshaw to live with her unmarried because she believes personal ties stronger and more sincere than social or religious ones. Ford plainly intends to show us that Katya's self-explanation is suspect. He proceeds by introducing, for purposes of invidious comparison, a minor character—little Kitty Langham, Katya's niece, who has never spoken. Her silence, according to Katya, is "a sort of dramatic display," revealing a "jealously affectionate" nature. And, as Ford prepares to use Kitty to Katya's discredit, he makes Katya phrase the general question: "The desire to be made a fuss of, to occupy the *whole* mind of some person or of many persons, to cause one's power to be felt— are these not motives very human?" (p. 100). Very soon Katya undertakes to cure Kitty. Her method is feigned indifference; and when she embraces Grimshaw in the reunion scene, the method succeeds. Parting the couple, Kitty speaks: "Nobody must be loved but me." Katya repeats Kitty's words, and exclaims, "Oh, poor child," because "in the words the child had given to her she recognized the torture of her own passion" (p. 114). Thus Ford presents Katya as she claims to be and Katya as, supposedly, she really is. While she claims to value trustfulness above all, she is really jealous and possessive.

Ford's use of Kitty to unmask Katya, and thereby condemn her personal ethic, is in its way no less abstract and no more plausible than Grimshaw's allegiance to the "amenities." The psychology of Kitty's malady and cure is embarrassingly dubious, but, even if it were not, the points of resemblance between Kitty and Katya are too many and too regularly emphasized to give the illusion of life.

Although the meeting with the priest presents no difficulties in characterization, here again, and in a more literal sense, the novelist's mirror reflects no apparently natural scene, but a stage that is all too plainly "set." Grimshaw's meeting with the priest is followed by too many other chance encounters, with passers-by who prompt, one by one, the various points of the priest's discourse. Then the conclusion of the whole dialectic stretches toward importance but falls into flat, mechanical rhetoric. The priest concludes his plea for emotional expression with the words:

> "Go out into the world; help all that you may; induce all that you may to go into the right paths. Bring one unto the other, that mutual comprehension may result. That is the way of Christian fellowship; that is the way to bring about the peace of God on earth" (p. 222).

A Call survives these moments. It survives them in large part because of Dudley Leicester and, surprising as the assertion may seem at first, Katya Lascarides. The sequence transporting Dudley from the security of his wife's company to the anonymous confrontation in Etta Hudson's front hall is skillfully (and comically) executed, and the telephone call itself is convincingly prepared for. Dudley's indecorous impulses point toward his indiscretion with Etta; his anxiety and fear over those impulses foreshadow his immediate and extreme remorse. In a sense, Dudley expects the call: as soon as the telephone rings, he feels quite certain that he has committed a crime. The voice at the other end of the wire seems to function as the objective counterpart of his own conscience.

Even after he withdraws into madness, Dudley continues, one way and another, to enliven the novel. Etta Hudson, for example, becomes his vigorously eccentric champion. And Grimshaw does at last commit himself to a struggle as, with Pauline, he tries to keep up appearances in the face of Dudley's illness. He helps Pauline entertain representative members of Mayfair while Ellida and a male nurse pretend to include Dudley's "passive form" in "animated conversations" (p. 195). All this time, Grimshaw really suffers, in his dread of exposure, his resentment of the strain of hypocrisy.

As for Katya, she would compel only our disbelief save that Ford has given her an "appearance" as well as a "reality." And Katya as she claims to be is credible. Her reactions, as she tells them, to the news of her illegitimacy form a convincing pattern of shock, resentment, and eventual adjustment to a very much altered view of the world. On the level of "appearance," Katya's present is consistent with her past, and she gains from us the sympathy that comes from understanding. The fact that she does not finally emerge as a "disagreeable personality" becomes a matter of considerable importance at the end of the novel.

Significantly, the best parts of A Call, those in which Ford displays a recognizable increase in imaginative power, compose a second story within the frame of the first. In the second story, meaning is implicit rather than explicit, a matter of symbol and "natural" personality rather than exposition and contrived psychology. The two stories do essentially reinforce each other, though not on all points. And the evidence suggests that Ford was finally moving close to a unity of theme and narrative, even though he could not yet fully achieve it.

The basis of the second story is a different conception not only of Katya but of Grimshaw as well. Explicitly, Grimshaw is a man who cannot fulfill the role he chooses for himself, the role of the man of honor, of the English gentleman who holds his feelings firmly in harness. Explicitly, Grimshaw cannot help loving both Pauline and Katya, and he continues to love Pauline even after her marriage to Dudley. On the implicit level of meaning, however, Grimshaw is a man who not only wants to but does hold to his ideal code of action—until the very end of the novel. In refusing to meet Katya's challenge to lawlessness, he acts honorably; at the same time, he refuses to accept a sexual invitation. Katya is "dark and passionate," possessed of a "southern nature." Her friends had

found her retirement after her broken engagement a "little out of
the picture" because it gave her the "aspect" of a "nun," or at least
of assuming a "cloistral frame of mind" (p. 23)—and they are
apparently right. For when Katya meets Grimshaw in the scene
of their reunion, she embraces him and "without will or control"
entreats him: "Oh, take me! Take me! Now! For good . . . ." (p.
113).

In response, Grimshaw at first is plainly happy to find that
Katya has overcome her old "loathing," her old revulsion from him.
"It's heaven," he says, "to know that you've grown out of it. It
has been hell to bear the thought. . . ." (p. 119). But then, the
meeting abruptly ends in discord. Katya refuses to change her terms
of union and Grimshaw again refuses to meet them. He explains
to Katya—and the explanation contradicts the delight he has just
expressed in her love for him—"You've strengthened me in my
motive. If you had shuddered at me as you did on that day years
ago, I think I should have given in by now" (p. 123). Katya's reply,
"If I'd repulsed you, you'd have given in?" (p. 123) remains unanswered and provocative. For by the end of the reunion Grimshaw
has appeared not as one personality but as two. He is a man who
loves Pauline and Katya and wants to possess them both. But he
also is a man who shies away from passion, shies away, particularly,
from the passion Katya is so ready to offer him.

The first conception of Grimshaw's character continues to be
carried on in the explicit level of the novel. The second is confirmed
in still another meeting with Katya, when Grimshaw visits her to
ask her to care for Dudley Leicester. At first, Katya is willing, but
she changes her mind when she realizes the extent to which Grimshaw is possessed by the fate of his friend. She scolds him jealously,
in no uncertain terms:

> "No wonder you can't give in to me if you've got to be think-
> ing of him all the time. Well, put it how you will, I have done
> with him, and I've done with you. Go your own idiotic ways
> together. I've done with you." And with her hands stretched
> down in front of her she snapped the handle of her parasol, her
> face drawn and white. She looked down at the two pieces con-
> temptuously, and threw them against the iron-bolted, oak
> church door (p. 253).

Here Katya rejects the whole code of conventional values which the "iron-bolted, oak church door" stands for. And she also rejects Grimshaw as a suitor, for the picture, so close to Conrad's habitual portrayal of meetings between men and women, is obviously a symbolic one of sexual failure—of inadequacy on the part of the man and contempt on the part of the woman.

In the light of his implicit characterization, Grimshaw's relationship to Dudley yields considerable meaning. For an identification clearly exists between the two men. Indeed, Grimshaw has virtually made Dudley his creature. He counselled him throughout their years together at Winchester and Oxford. He turned him into a "model landlord." He kept him from marrying Etta Hudson, by occupying him with "the healthy sort of things that keep a man off women" (p. 163). And, of course, his interference later makes it certain that Dudley will not become Etta's lover. His call leaves Dudley overcome by guilt, sitting "dishevelled and dejected, as if all his joints had been broken" (p. 77).

Grimshaw, then, shapes Dudley to the same gentlemanly pattern of behavior he chooses for himself—even to the extent of preventing Dudley from giving way to passion. For Etta Hudson extends to Dudley the same kind of emotional challenge Katya offers Grimshaw. Ford, in fact, exaggerates Etta's attractions with a good deal of humor. Etta is "red-lipped, deep-voiced, black-haired, large, warm, scented, and utterly uncontrollable" (p. 52). On the fateful night of the call, she draws Dudley along "as in a picture a nymph might lead away a stripling into scented obscurities into leafy woods" (p. 63).

In contrast to both Katya and Etta, Pauline is "tiny," with "porcelain cheeks" and a brow like "soft and translucent china" (p. 38). She looks like a "newly awakened and wondering child" (p. 38); her tongue goes "perpetually, with its infantile gaiety" (p. 195). In Etta Hudson's devastating opinion, she is a "little wax saint, isn't she, got up to look like a Gaiety girl?" (p. 154) Dudley feels "safe" only when he is with Pauline. And Pauline's brittle and childish appearance suggests that she represents "safety" for Grimshaw as well. On the implicit level of meaning, that is, Grimshaw seeks to escape from experience in all his relationships. He refuses to meet Katya's challenge; he tries to make Dudley over into his own impassive image; and, despite later and supposedly frank statements to the contrary, he really seems to want just what he first says he wants of Pauline—"to watch her going through the lancers with that little mouth just open, and the little hand just holding out her skirt, and a little, tender expression of joy" (p. 16).

Finally, Grimshaw's convincing struggle to maintain appearances in the face of Dudley's madness arises from motives more personal than his stated respect for the "amenities." By concealing Dudley's madness, he tries to conceal its cause. He tries to maintain the fiction that Dudley was not attracted to Etta Hudson and that he himself is not, by virtue of identification with Dudley, guilty of involvement in a sexual relationship. Grimshaw, moreover, is afraid of what Dudley may yet do. He fears that Dudley will turn on Pauline, despite her assurance to the contrary. He also fears, with no more ground in external reality, that Katya will attack Pauline. In his own mind, Grimshaw not only sees passion as indecorous but links it with physical violence. Hence his anxiety to separate Dudley, and himself, from the life of "impulse" and of "instinct."

Explicitly, Ford brings his novel to an unhappy conclusion: Grimshaw marries Katya simply to take himself away from Pauline. Or, as Ford puts it in his epilogue, by "succumbing" to Katya, Grimshaw commits the "final folly of this particular affair." But Grimshaw's implicit characterization and Katya's as well bring to the novel's ending an impression of fulfillment in contrast to the frustration Ford himself insisted on. For Katya emerges, in part, as sympathetic rather than "disagreeable." Her passionate reunion with Grimshaw suggests that she is at least capable of loving generously rather than possessively; and hints, further, that she may have the power to release Grimshaw from his emotional constraint. By submitting to Katya, Grimshaw at last enters into experience. Or, to describe his fate in terms of Ford's earlier novels of love, Grimshaw is forced to choose "life," to act in spite of guilt and fear, to risk maturity.

The second story in *A Call* thus reinforces the novel's dialectic. Katya, with her capacity for passion, after all represents a way of life that allows the expression of emotion. On the implicit level of meaning, the demands she has made on Grimshaw become reasonable rather than excessive. Her unorthodox challenge has been part of an effort to induce her diffident suitor to abandon his inhibitions and partake of human experience. On the implicit level, in other words, Katya's values are essentially the same as those set forth in the dialectic. Grimshaw commits his "folly" not when he "succumbs" to her but when, for so long, he resists her.

Ford himself seems to have been unaware of the relationship between his two stories. Probably he was unaware of the very existence of his second story. He planned, as he tells us, to make Grimshaw a "meddlesome fool" and Katya a "disagreeable personality." But as the novel finally shows, the designs of the conscious moralist repeatedly gave way to the realizations of the "natural" and, very likely, unconscious psychologist. Ford could neither understand nor sympathize with a hero who professed an impersonal allegiance to "civilization" and a heroine who refused to marry simply to prove her "power." But he could, both plausibly and sympathetically, intuit the behavior of a hero who was so afraid of love that he sought to escape it and a heroine who tried to arouse his passion.

Despite the discrepancies between the work of the explicit moralist and that of the intuitive psychologist, despite very obvious areas of ignorance, *A Call* is the best novel Ford published before the first war. And it is a very promising novel. I think it probable that Ford did consciously understand the more obvious plights of Dudley Leicester and Etta Hudson. As a gentleman, Dudley is outraged by Etta's flirtations with the third footman and the farrier's son; later, as a husband "conveniently" married to an "infantile" woman, he is susceptible to Etta's seductive charms, and his exacting conscience makes him liable to an extreme reaction of guilt. Etta's frank approach to love and her resolve to "get" Dudley (p. 181) are also clearly conceived. And both Dudley and Etta are successfully integrated into the moral point of view of the novel. With various changes, they both appear in *The Good Soldier*—as Edward Ashburnham and the Spanish dancer who took him to Antibes.

Even in his handling of Katya and Grimshaw, Ford made progress toward his mature work. Katya is a fuller development of the heroines of *The Inheritors* and *The Benefactor*. The dimensionist girl has no local habitation, not even a name, and Clara Brede, while she possesses a family background, enjoys only a very limited and indistinct relationship with George Moffat. But Katya possesses both a past and a present, and Ford was able to carry her beyond a final and rather inarticulate farewell to her reluctant suitor. Katya's anger and jealousy are credible enough; they arise, on the implicit level of the novel, after Grimshaw has failed to respond to the love she is ready to offer him. Grimshaw, who takes his place in the succession of Etchingham Granger, George Moffat, and Don Collar Kelleg, is also rendered in greater detail.[7] Implicitly, Ford was able in *A Call* to place his diffident hero not in just one or two but in a whole series of consistent personal relationships—with Katya, with Pauline, with Dudley, with Etta. Ford was, in brief, learning to imagine the responses of his hero as well as his heroine to a variety of contingencies. In some ways, Katya prefigures Nancy Rufford, in others, Valentine Wannop; Grimshaw's attraction to "safety," his aversion to passion, his identification with a friend, his desperate effort to maintain appearances when that friend breaks with convention—all have their counterparts in Dowell's pattern of action in *The Good Soldier*.

II

His early novels show us that Ford was, on the one hand, an objective observer of the contemporary and historical English scene. He perceived corruption in all sorts of high and apparently pure places. And as a novelist he was motivated by a didactic impulse to expose vanity, greed, hypocrisy. He wanted to teach his readers that colonial schemes could be vicious; that "justice" could be

---

7. For a similar view of Ford's heroes in his early novels of love, see Thomas Moser's "Towards *The Good Soldier*—Discovery of a Sexual Theme," which appeared after this study was completed (*Dædalus*, Proceedings of the American Academy of Arts and Sciences, Vol. 92, No. 2 [Spring, 1963], 312-325). While Moser does not focus on the evolution of Ford's moral values, he too finds Ford gradually arriving at an understanding of his heroes' sexual inadequacies. He discusses *The Shifting of the Fire* specifically, and revealingly, in a Freudian light. And, at the same time that he acknowledges the artistic inferiority of *The Panel*, he makes a case for including it, along with *The Benefactor*, *An English Girl*, and *A Call*, as a precursor of *The Good Soldier*.

bought; that artistic talent was compatible with ruthless material ambition; that the leisure class shirked its social responsibilities, that marriages of convenience were an outrage to human sensibilities. Even his historical romances were, in their remote and simplified way, didactic allegories. The sins of the English present were spawned by those of the English past. Tudor politics had also been corrupt and bureaucracy had followed hard upon the victory at Bosworth.

On the other hand, Ford was also a psychological novelist. He frequently turned from his broad social concerns to moments of internal crisis. From the beginning of his career, he showed a disposition to create certain subjective states of feeling—of resentment, anger, outrage, and defiance, of solitude, inadequacy, anxiety, dread, guilt, weariness, and hopelessness. He traced the genesis of Katya Lascarides' rebellion against convention; he followed Etchingham Granger's hesitant and fearful progress toward the dimensionist girl who awaited him in the antique mansion in the Faubourg Saint Germain.

Both as social critic and as psychologist, Ford had much to learn. He began with no firm ethical principles by which to measure society, whether contemporary or historical. He wanted both to exonerate and to condemn his romantic heroes, both to support and to overturn traditional ideals of honor. And his subjective states of feeling, as *The Benefactor* alone reminds us, were frequently abstract; he had to explore them, to learn to link them with concrete human situations and to order them according to consistent and plausible patterns of character and action.

The process of moral and psychological discovery was slow and difficult. Ford frequently skirted the very areas of his material that, in retrospect, seem most promising. In his Tudor trilogy, he failed to involve his protagonist in a major struggle until the very end of his work. In *The Benefactor*, he began to explore the characters of his hero and heroine in his last scene. And even when he did reach an ethical compromise between the extremes of tradition and self-expression, his novels continue to reveal the moralist at odds with the psychologist. In *The 'Half Moon'*, he achieved intellectual consistency at the expense of characterization. Similarly, he filled the foreground of *The Young Lovell* with a monumental, and obscurant, mass of medieval detail. And he seems, of course, to have remained consistently ignorant of many of the implications of *A Call*. There, within the conscious bonds of his dialectic, a whole second story struggled toward expression.

Ford's ethical contradictions, his various evasions, and his areas of ignorance go far, I think, toward explaining the frequently indifferent quality of his early novels. Yet this accumulation of evidence tempts me further, in the effort to find some still more fundamental reasons why Ford's fulfillment as a novelist was so long delayed. From here on my argument will be, quite frankly, speculative, and will begin by digressing into the memoirs and prefaces.

In *Ancient Lights and Certain New Reflections* (1911), which he dedicates to his daughters, Ford writes:

> This book, in short, is full of inaccuracies as to facts, but its accuracy as to impressions is absolute. For the facts, when you have a little time to waste, I should suggest that you go through this book carefully, noting the errors. To the one of you who succeeds in finding the largest number I will cheerfully present a copy of the ninth edition of the Encyclopædia Britannica, so that you may still further perfect yourself in the hunting out of errors. [. . .] I don't really deal in facts, I have for facts a most profound contempt.[8]

The voice is insistent.

It speaks again, to a different end, in the preface to *No More Parades*.

> In this novel the events, such as it treats of, are vouched for by myself. [. . .] There is, I think, not one word in it which records any opinions or words of mine as being my words or opinions. I believe I may say that, as to the greater part of such public matters as are here discussed, I have no opinions at all. After seven or eight years I have been unable to form any. I present therefore only what I observed or heard.[9]

---

8. Ford Madox Hueffer, "Dedication," *Ancient Lights and Certain New Reflections: Being the Memories of a Young Man* (London: Chapman & Hall, 1911), p. xv. Published in the United States as *Memories and Impressions: A Study in Atmospheres* (New York & London: Harper, 1911).

9. "Dedication," *No More Parades* (New York: Albert & Charles Boni, 1925), pp. v-vi.

Ford's ambivalent attitude toward the diurnal world of facts and figures is obvious enough. In *Ancient Lights* he scorns reality and implies that his "impressions" as a creative writer are more true than literal truth. But in the preface to *No More Parades* he claims to speak not as a creative artist but only as a scrupulous observer of what has actually happened. By implication he celebrates things as they are rather than things as the imagination would have them.

What concerns me chiefly here, however, is not the contradiction between the statements in *Ancient Lights* and in *No More Parades,* but rather the fundamental sameness of intention that I believe underlies them both—an intention that may account for their curious note of insistence. As he begins a book of "memoirs," Ford announces his scorn for facts. In his preface to a novel, he presents himself merely as a reporter. In either case, he disclaims responsibility; he separates himself from what he has written. He announces, in effect, that he will not anywhere reveal himself.

I am not going to contradict him altogether. Or rather, I am going to look only a little beyond the smoke screen of Ford the scornful artist and the mere reporter in order to find Ford the man. For all his disclaimers, Ford was, I think, a very personal novelist. In his fiction he does to some extent reveal himself.

Whatever their outward differences, Ford's protagonists are fundamentally alike in motivation. The diffident hero is insecure. He is ridden by guilt and shame. Though his loyalty to his code of honor is not insincere—he believes his code is morally good—his ethical values serve to excuse his timidity, his fear of engaging in experience. And his psyche is in certain ways repeated in the second variation of Ford's "story." There Ford *externalizes* guilt and shame. He presents a brave hero who is not, at least initially, afraid of what he has done or may yet do. But people attribute shameful motives to him, bear false witness against him, sometimes put him literally on trial for his life. Both heroes are therefore victims—the first of his own guilty conscience, the second of a malevolent society—and both seek either to maintain or to establish their innocence. For they are, finally, egoists who would be quite beyond reproach. They demand of themselves a pattern of conduct that will not only make them superior to ordinary men, but raise them above the very limitations of human nature.

I suggest that Ford's protagonists reflect himself. His very preoccupation with his "story," his disposition to tell it, in one variation or the other, again and again and again is a compelling reason to suppose an intimate tie between the novelist and his heroes. Support for the supposition appears in the autobiographical material, for, despite their disregard for factual accuracy, Ford's memoirs comprise a series of personal revelations.

From *Ancient Lights and Certain New Reflections* to *It Was the Nightingale* (1933), Ford assumes various *personae*; he plays the Sussex farmer and the wealthy man about town, the carefree student at Bonn and the weary editor in Paris. But no matter where he sets his stage or what particular role he chooses for the moment to adopt, Ford's conception of himself remains constant. Consider, for example, the following excerpt from *It Was the Nightingale*:

> It was during one of these festivals [his Friday dances in Paris] that I had my first experience of Prohibition. I was dancing with a girl of seventeen who appeared to be enthusiastic and modest. And suddenly—amazingly—she dropped right through my arms and lay on the floor like a corpse. I was, as it were, shattered. I thought she had died of heart disease.
>
> No one in the room stopped dancing. They were all Americans and nearly all from the Middle West. The girl's mother came from another room and, helped by her brother, carried the girl away. She expressed no particular concern and hardly any vexation. I had never seen a girl—I don't believe I had ever seen a woman or even a man—in such a condition before.[10]

Ford is conventional and therefore naïve: he expects young girls to be sober; he has never heard of the kick in bathtub booze. He also is susceptible to shock and strong reaction, and he expresses the unmistakable plaintiveness of a reasonable man adrift in an unreasonable world.

Frequently, that world is not only incomprehensible but uncomprehending as well. The memoirs go on. Edgar Lee Masters mistakes Ford for a janitor; Mrs. Major So and So, for a man who never reads. The American Women's Club of Paris mistake him for a Communist—they burn the second number of his *transatlantic*

---

10. *It Was the Nightingale* (Philadelphia & London: Lippincott, 1933), pp. 330-331.

review. Conrad flies at his throat when, for the best of reasons, he interrupts Conrad's work. Joyce fails to meet him for dinner. Gertrude Stein does not heed him, as he pants in the wake of her Model T, hoping to talk about art. Financiers give him disastrous financial advice. Golfers scold him for playing golf. A stranger on the telephone warns him against the malice of Hemingway *père*. Hemingway *père* on the telephone extends a sincere offer of friendship and hospitality. Pound tells him to hire a Russian colonel as a sub-editor. He does, and Pound is outraged.

The rather shy, inept, well-meaning personage of the memoirs—he goes by the names of Huffer, Hoofer, and Hweffer—makes no excessive demands on us. He asks for our sympathy, to be sure, but he also amuses us with his luckless progress through the capitals and byways of the Western world. Ford is a comic raconteur, in other words, who cuts his conception of himself to meet the demands of art. His bid for compassion is controlled, as is his tacit indictment of "enemies." Still, if we disregard the detachment that comes from comedy, Huffer-Hoofer-Hweffer is essentially like the heroes of Ford's first "story"—insecure, threatened, and, however implicitly, anxious to say that, though he is punished, he is nonetheless innocent. In that pattern, repeated in the novels and memoirs alike, we would seem to have the reflection of Ford's own preoccupations and needs.

These suppositions might simply be gossip, better confined to coffee time—were it not that they help account for Ford's strengths and weaknesses as a novelist. I have already suggested that Ford's formal difficulties are largely symptomatic, that they proceed from his inconsistent moral and emotional attitudes toward his material and from his various evasions and areas of ignorance of psychological complexity. I suggest now that these attitudes and these evasions are influenced by his own psychic need to banish insecurity and achieve self-vindication.

Ford's contrary, and extreme, moral positions both offer complete self-vindication to their followers. The brave protagonist need only keep to his exacting standards of conduct. If he dies, his death serves as a supreme reproach to his tormentors and revilers. A scrupulous code of honor serves the diffident hero much less efficiently. He *feels* guilty, and because his accusers dwell within, he may silence them only by summoning sufficient courage to discard his gentlemanly code. In effect, he is challenged to throw off the inhibitions of his conscience and to substitute for his insecurity aggressive self-expression, so that his impulses will be no longer shameful but good, both the motive and the sanction of his actions.

For years really, Ford fails to develop the first form of his "story"—a "story" that leads him eventually to the creation of John Dowell, a hero who is indisputably guilty, who fails to banish doubt and shame. In *The Inheritors* Ford presents a diffident hero who betrays the human community for a woman. Explicitly the novel condemns his irresponsibility, but implicitly it shows a disposition to criticize him, not for choosing the woman, but simply for failing to choose her earlier and more decisively than he does. In both *The Benefactor* and *An English Girl* Ford guides his heroes—who also are diffident—to accept rigorous traditional codes of honor. But the very last scene of each novel challenges these heroes with crises that seem to demand not responsible social conduct but free self-expression. And there Ford drops his "story." He brings George Moffat and Don Collar Kelleg, as it were, to the brink of Dowell's disaster, and there he hesitates. In *A Call* he writes with more audacity and explicitly condemns his hero—yet, implicitly, he draws another Grimshaw, who does not merely voice his approval of a traditional ethic but lives according to that ethic as well.

All these novels bespeak, I think, a common disposition in their creator. In *The Benefactor* and *An English Girl* Ford withholds judgment on his diffident heroes. In *The Inheritors* and *A Call*, he implicitly justifies their actions. Consciously or unconsciously, and whatever the cost in evasion or inconsistency, Ford is concerned either to guard or to protest his heroes' innocence. And this disposition is even more pronounced in a number of the early historical novels. In *The Fifth Queen Crowned,* in at least a section of *The Portrait,* and in *The New Humpty-Dumpty,* Ford draws incredibly brave and good protagonists who triumph completely over externalized guilt and shame.

I have, obviously enough, restricted my suppositions about Ford the man to general ones. I am wary of drawing more particular parallels between Ford and his characters. My reasons are two and, although I consider either sufficient, I should like to set them both down here. The first is simply my slight acquaintance with the facts of Ford's life. In Douglas Goldring, Ford has had a casual and a partisan biographer. Many of Goldring's data require revision, and he is more concerned to defend Ford than to explain him. He attributes Ford's unreliability, for example, simply to the creative artist's yearning to turn a good story into a better one. Violet Hunt's volume of memoirs, *The Flurried Years*,[11] and Stella Bowen's, *Drawn from Life*,[12] may bring us closer to the real Ford. Yet even these accounts, colored as they are by markedly different sensibilities, leave many questions unanswered; Ford still needs a thorough and judicious biographer.

My second reason for eschewing more particular hypotheses about Ford relates to the creative process itself. Even when the novelist works intuitively or unconsciously, he may not, I think, simply project himself into his characters. He may also—unknowingly—fashion his heroes after models in the external world. Mimesis, then, and self-projection may both combine to make a novel. But where do we draw the line between the contribution of one creative process and the other? I can't answer with certainty; I simply think that line is best drawn with caution—and end my suppositions at the common ground where the diffident hero and the brave one and Huffer, Hoofer, and Hweffer meet. Even if I knew a good deal about Ford's life, I doubt that I would find certain clues that his own personality conformed to the very specifically realized patterns of motivation that guide the destinies of, say, John Dowell or Edward Ashburnham. "I want to make it clear," Pirandello writes, "that the inherent torment of my spirit is one thing, a torment which I can legitimately—provided that it be organic—reflect in a character . . . the realized work . . . is another thing."[13] The fairly sharp distinction between "one thing" and "another" may well hold for Ford.

Criticism goes, I think, only so far. It can point to the major flaws in Ford's early novels and it can, as I have tried to do,

---

11. London: Hurst and Blackett, 1926. Published in the United States as *I Have This to Say* (New York: Boni and Liveright, 1926).

12. London: Collins, 1941.

13. *Naked Masks: Five Plays by Luigi Pirandello,* ed. Eric Bentley (New York: Dutton, 1958), p. 369.

speculate on the reasons for them; but it cannot explain the eventual maturity that produced *The Good Soldier* and the four volumes of *Parade's End.*

The rest of Ford's development toward control of his contemporary material remains, quite simply, inexplicable. When he returned to his "story," at the end of 1913, he wrote not another faulty and inconsistent apprentice work but an unequivocal masterpiece. At some point between the publication of *A Call* and the day some four years later when he began *The Good Soldier* he arrived, in ways unknown, at an understanding of his diffident romantic hero. He learned to present him with sympathy and still judge him according to his newly evolved scheme of moral values. And he was finally able to utilize the materials that energized his imagination to convey a profound criticism of traditional English society.

CHAPTER 4

The Good Soldier

I

AFTER FORD's early fiction, *The Good Soldier* is both familiar and strange. It is so much like the other novels; it is so much better than they are. There is little need, now, to plead for its excellence. But there is still room for analysis—of its technique, of its psychology, of its vision of life. Even Mark Schorer's admirable Introduction to the 1951 edition, by far the best discussion of the novel to date, just begins to explore its intricate and inviting ways.[1]

In Chapter II, Part One, the narrator John Dowell remarks:

---

1. Mark Schorer, "An Interpretation," *The Good Soldier: A Tale of Passion* (New York: Knopf, 1951), pp. v-xv. This essay appeared in earlier form as "The Good Novelist in *The Good Soldier*" in both *The Princeton University Library Chronicle*, IX (April, 1948), 128-133, and *Horizon*, XX (August, 1949), 132-138.

My strong preference for Schorer's essay after so many others have appeared (for a list and summaries of most of them, see Joseph Wiesenfarth's "Criticism and the Semiosis of *The Good Soldier*" in *Modern Fiction Studies*, IX [Spring, 1963], 39-49)—my continuing preference for Schorer's essay may require a word of explanation. The fact is that Schorer does see that Dowell is a self-deceiving narrator and Schorer does link his deception with his sexual inadequacy and its attendant need for self-defense. To my mind, then, Schorer points the way to a reasonable reading of the novel. And to combat his beginnings, as so many critics have subsequently done, is to see *The Good Soldier* as unnecessarily and unjustifiably puzzling or inconclusive. (After his summaries, Wiesenfarth writes, "It is still probable that Dowell's version of the facts is true . . . it is as equally [sic] probable that he is in error.")

"I don't know how it is best to put this thing down [. . .]. So I shall just imagine myself for a fortnight or so at one side of the fireplace of a country cottage, with a sympathetic soul opposite me. And I shall go on talking."[2] As Dowell "talks," casually, reminiscently, the novel moves back and forth between two planes of chronological development. The first is time present, in which Dowell speaks. He begins his narrative early in 1914, ten days after the death of his friend Edward Ashburnham. As he proceeds, he mentions that a month, six months, and finally eighteen more months have passed. From the vantage point, or rather points, of time present, Dowell reconstructs time past. There is a certain rough order in his reconstruction. He speaks first of various crucial events that took place in August, 1904, at Nauheim. Then he shifts back farther in time and describes his own life to the day in August, 1913, when his wife Florence died. He then transfers his attention to Edward and Leonora Ashburnham, recounting their lives to the autumn of 1913. At the end of the novel, the gap between time present and time past is closed. And within his planes of time, Dowell free-associates. His subject of the moment reminds him of other events, so that he moves freely within his whole chronological range.

Ford's art is thus one of surprise and sudden contrast.[3] He writes his scenes briefly, in a paragraph or a page or two. He focuses upon his characters in typical attitudes or moments of action—Florence smiling over her shoulder at Nauheim, Edward swinging his polo pony 'round, Leonora crying in the arms of a lover she cannot enjoy—then moves on immediately to other times, other events. He also reveals much of his most important information incidentally. Dowell describes Edward's suicide as an afterthought, at the very end of the novel. He mentions Edward's affair with a Spanish dancer as an explanation of his financial reverses. He uses the death of Maisie Maidan, another woman Edward loved, to fix the precise date of a sight-seeing excursion.

---

2. *The Good Soldier* (New York: Knopf, 1951), p. 12. All subsequent references in the text will be to this edition.

3. John A. Meixner has commented on this aspect of Ford's technique in *Ford Madox Ford's Novels*, pp. 170-171. A shorter version of Meixner's chapter on *The Good Soldier* appeared as "The Saddest Story" in *The Kenyon Review*, XXII (Spring, 1960), 234-264.

In his criticism Ford frequently said that he employed chronological dislocation and distortion of emphasis to achieve verisimilitude. "Life does not say to you: In 1914 my next door neighbour, Mr. Slack, erected a greenhouse and painted it with Cox's green aluminium paint. . . . If you think about the matter you will remember, in various unordered pictures, how one day Mr. Slack appeared in his garden and contemplated the wall of his house."[4] There is no doubt about this. Life does not reach us with the coherence and predictability of every article in the *Reader's Digest*. And *The Good Soldier*, with its brief and tantalizing glimpses of character, conversation, and action, gives the effect of life.

Yet, as Albert J. Guerard has taught us, the impressionist "game" is far more complex and "more sinister."[5] Dislocation and distortion achieve verisimilitude; they also force us to participate in a novel, to organize the discrete and unordered. What sort of man, for example, is Edward Ashburnham? Hero or sentimentalist? Libertine or elder brother? Reading an impressionist novel, we feel, as Guerard has put it, "a provisional bafflement in the face of experience which turns out to be more complicated than we ever would have dreamed."[6] The truth, since great art is finally free from the irrelevancies of life, is richly present in *The Good Soldier*— but we find it only by indirection and involvement. As Ford's narrative ebbs and flows, and turns back again and again upon itself (to Florence's death, say, or to Edward's love for his ward Nancy Rufford), first impressions are altered, often even contradicted. We must organize, and must organize material about which we come to feel deeply.

The novel begins:

> This is the saddest story I have ever heard. We had known the Ashburnhams for nine seasons of the town of Nauheim with an extreme intimacy—or, rather, with an acquaintanceship as loose and easy and yet as close as a good glove's with your hand. My wife and I knew Captain and Mrs. Ashburnham as well as it was possible to know anybody, and yet, in another sense, we knew nothing at all about them. This is, I believe, a state of things

---

4. *Joseph Conrad*, pp. 180-181.
5. *Conrad the Novelist*, p. 126.
6. *Ibid.*, p. 127.

only possible with English people of whom, till today, when I sit down to puzzle out what I know of this sad affair, I knew nothing whatever. Six months ago I had never been to England, and, certainly, I had never sounded the depths of an English heart. I had known the shallows (p. 3).

With these opening sentences, quiet, serious, sonorous, and carefully qualified, Ford presents us with a narrator who has seen and heard and "sounded the depths." Dowell's voice will be a versatile one, capable of ranging from the exquisitely lyrical "It was true sunshine; the true music; the true plash of the fountains from the mouth of stone dolphins" (p. 7) to the humorously banal "Fellows come in and tell the most extraordinarily gross stories—so gross that they will positively give you a pain" (p. 10). Dowell is a vivid storyteller, and in all its moods his voice compels attention.

This Philadelphia gentleman, with his title deeds of wampum, is a satiric instrument as well. He is not literally a visitor to the scene of the action, as Gulliver is to Lilliput or Lien Chi Altangi to eighteenth-century London. But in Ford's hands he plays virtually the same role of astonished traveler. He is a stranger to the very American and European society in which he has lived all his life because he has always believed in appearances. He has assumed that people practiced the morals they preached and that their external aspect of being "good people" (p. 34) represented their true characters. As the novel opens, circumstances have just forced him to exchange a portion of his habitual naïveté for a more realistic view of the world. Under the pressure of shock, he tells much of his story in a tone of amazement or wonder. After Leonora tells him, for example, that she once tried to take a lover, he exclaims: "I don't know; I don't know; was that last remark of hers the remark of a harlot, or is it what every decent woman, county family or not county family, thinks at the bottom of her heart? Or thinks all the time, for the matter of that?" (p. 9).

His narrator's naïveté allows Ford important artistic advantages in The Good Soldier. Through Dowell, Ford assumes attitudes that emphasize the absurdity of human behavior and insist on the discrepancy that generally obtains between aspiration and accomplishment. Yet the attitudes are, as it were, absorbed by the narrator's personality. Ford is still a social critic and historian, but no longer so at the expense of his art. His didactic interests do not override characterization and narrative as they did, for example, in the Tudor trilogy or in parts of *A Call.*

Dowell is, furthermore, a double-edged weapon; Ford uses his narrator to ridicule society, and he also renders him ridiculous. Dowell's claim to wisdom, to have "sounded the depths," quickly becomes in itself absurd. In one sense, Dowell knows the facts of the story he tells. In another sense, he does not know them at all, for he cannot see their significance. Although Dowell is the narrator of *The Good Soldier,* its point of view in a larger sense is not after all limited to his vision of events, witness the following description of Maisie Maidan's death:

> [Leonora] had not cared to look round Maisie's rooms at first. Now, as soon as she came in, she perceived, sticking out beyond the bed, a small pair of feet in high-heeled shoes. Maisie had died in the effort to strap up a great portmanteau. She had died so grotesquely that her little body had fallen forward into the trunk, and it had closed upon her, like the jaws of a gigantic alligator. The key was in her hand. Her dark hair, like the hair of a Japanese, had come down and covered her body and her face.
>
> Leonora lifted her up—she was the merest featherweight—and laid her on the bed with her hair about her. She was smiling, as if she had just scored a goal in a hockey match. You understand she had not committed suicide. Her heart had just stopped. I saw her, with the long lashes on the cheeks, with the smile about the lips, with the flowers all about her. The stem of a white lily rested in her hand so that the spike of flowers was upon her shoulder. She looked like a bride in the sunlight of the mortuary candles that were all about her, and the white coifs of the two nuns that knelt at her feet with the faces hidden might have been two swans that were to bear her away to kissing-kindness land, or wherever it is. Leonora showed her to me. She would not let either of the others see her. She wanted, you know, to spare poor dear Edward's feelings. He never could bear the sight of a corpse. And, since she never gave him an idea that Maisie had written to her, he imagined that the death had been the most natural thing in the world. He soon got over it. Indeed, it was the one affair of his about which he never felt much remorse (pp. 75-76).

Here Dowell is a witness who faces the fact of death and simply does not care. His tone is that of a gossip, enthusiastic and eager to convey sensational and intimate detail, but otherwise empty of emotion. He is indifferent to Maisie, to Leonora—indifferent, too, to Edward's indifference.

Yet Dowell's is a mind that not only notes surface detail but also makes rapid and varied associations. And virtually through the imagery alone the passage makes a strong and meaningful statement of its event. Maisie has died abruptly, head over heels, the trunk closing on her "like the jaws of a gigantic alligator." Death is cold, cruel, an ignominious accident, a sudden descent into indignity. Then, as the passage continues, Maisie is revealed smiling "as if she had just scored a goal in a hockey match." Her achievement is childish, and yet courageous—a diminutive whistle in the dark. And the unseen mortuary attendants complete the transformation from indignity and ugliness to decorum and beauty. Maisie is decked at the last in the trappings of romance and fairy tale. She appears as a bride, still smiling, among flowers, guarded within by nuns that "might have been two swans," and without by Leonora. Maisie's courage and the efforts of her attendants are very touching, and all the more so because they are futile: Maisie is nonetheless dead. If Dowell is blind to the emotional and moral import of his scene, we are not.

Dowell, then, frequently tells more than he knows. As the foregoing quotation suggests, Ford places his narrator in an ironic relationship with his narrative. Dowell habitually makes inappropriate responses to his story. He feels too little, or he feels too much. He makes inadequate judgments, or he derives unwarranted conclusions. All the incongruities are comic, but they are also part of the novel's meaning. For Dowell is, finally, much more than an arbitrary comic device; his individual failures in sensibility reveal an idiosyncratic yet consistently motivated personality. And as the local incongruities compose controlling patterns, his relationship to his narrative takes an unexpected turn and reveals the central paradox of the novel. The whole story of *The Good Soldier* is not just the substance of Dowell's narrative. It is the story of Dowell telling his story.

II

In the opening chapter, Dowell frequently speaks in elegiac tones. His is the "saddest story," and he mentions at once that his wife Florence and Edward Ashburnham are dead. His regret, however, is not for Florence or for Edward but for the end of the tranquil existence that he and his wife shared with the Ashburnhams:

> Supposing that you should come upon us sitting together at one of the little tables in front of the club house, let us say, at Homburg, taking tea of an afternoon and watching the miniature golf, you would have said that, as human affairs go, we were an extraordinarily safe castle. We were, if you will, one of those tall ships with the white sails upon a blue sea, one of those things that seem the proudest and the safest of all the beautiful and safe things that God has permitted the mind of men to frame. Where better could one take refuge? Where better?
>
> Permanence? Stability! I can't believe it's gone. I can't believe that that long, tranquil life, which was just stepping a minuet, vanished in four crashing days at the end of nine years and six weeks. Upon my word, yes, our intimacy was like a minuet, simply because on every possible occasion and in every possible circumstance we knew where to go, where to sit, which table we unanimously should choose; and we could rise and go, all four together, without a signal from any one of us, always to the music of the Kur orchestra, always in the temperate sunshine, or, if it rained, in discreet shelters (pp. 5-6).

Theirs was a life of scrupulous decorum and elaborate protocol. All "good people," they belonged to the leisurely and wealthy upper class of the Western world. And Edward belonged, particularly, to the landed class of England. He was "an excellent magistrate, a first-rate soldier, one of the best landlords, so they said, in Hampshire, England" (p. 11). Dowell is nostalgic as he looks to the past. And more, for he has just learned that his tranquil life was not what for nine years it seemed to be. Edward and Leonora were egregiously ill-matched. Edward, whom Dowell has always regarded as a paragon, indulged in affairs with many women. Florence was one of Edward's mistresses. These revelations call into question all Dowell's fundamental assumptions. Do people act morally or do they only pretend to do so, he asks. And if they only pretend, what constitutes reality? Their pretense or their actual behavior? Dowell continues his narration in an ostensible effort to answer these questions.

Through Part One of the novel, he quickly reveals that he is not a disinterested moralist. He repeatedly turns from his account of events to his own feelings about them and he forms a strong alliance with one of his protagonists. After his initial questions about the nature of reality, as he "talks" apparently casually, he sets up a series of sharp contrasts between his life before and after he met the Ashburnhams. Alone with Florence he had felt a "sense almost of nakedness—the nakedness that one feels on the sea-shore or in any great open space" (p. 21). He had been lonely, tired, unhappy—merely a "wanderer upon the face of public resorts" (p. 21). His attitude is puzzling, since Florence shared with the Ashburnhams many of the qualities Dowell values most. "She was bright; and she danced. She seemed to dance over the floors of castles and over seas and over and over the salons of modistes and over the *plages* of the Riviera" (p. 14). Florence, then, had "danced" before she joined the Ashburnhams in their "minuet." Her life had already been bright and ordered. But unlike the Ashburnhams, she offered Dowell no "refuge."

In contrast with his life with Florence, Dowell cites what proves to be, for him, a typical instance of a really good time. He describes a trip he made to the city of M—— with Florence *and* the Ashburnhams:

> I like catching the two-forty; I like the slow, smooth roll of the great big trains—and they are the best trains in the world! I like being drawn through the green country and looking at it through the clear glass of the great windows. Though, of course, the country isn't really green. The sun shines, the earth is blood red, and purple and red, and green and red. And the oxen in the ploughlands are bright varnished brown and black and blackish purple; and the peasants are dressed in the black and white of magpies; and there are great flocks of magpies too. [. . .] I was out for enjoyment. And I just enjoyed myself. It is so pleasant to be drawn along in front of the spectacular

towns with the peaked castle and the many double spires. In the sunlight, gleams come from the city—gleams from the glass of windows; from the gilt signs of apothecaries; from the ensigns of the student corps high up in the mountains; from the helmets of the funny little soldiers moving their stiff little legs in white linen trousers (pp. 41-43).

Dowell manages, to be sure, to communicate his enthusiasm. At the same time, the quality of his pleasure is curiously childlike. In the interior of the train, he is cut off from the real world, and he transforms it into a make-believe world: the "blood red, and purple and red, and green and red" earth might have been taken from a picture book, and the "varnished oxen" and the "funny little soldiers moving their stiff little legs" from a toy chest.

Dowell's requisites for happiness are apparently modest enough. But what, precisely, are they? Not a bright existence. Not traveling, even in good trains through pretty landscapes. Florence gave Dowell all those advantages. A clue to Dowell's needs, the needs that only the Ashburnhams can supply, appears at the end of the visit to M——. In the Rittersaal, before the draft of Luther's Protest, Florence praises the Reformation, then looks into Edward's eyes and touches his arm; Leonora takes Dowell by the wrist and hurries him down the winding stairs; for a moment, Dowell suspects that Leonora is jealous of Florence and Edward "of all people in the world!" (p. 45). Then Dowell looks at Leonora. "[Her eyes] were immense, were overwhelming, were like a wall of blue that shut me off from the rest of the world" (p. 45). Leonora explains her distress by saying that she is a Catholic, that Florence has just offended her religious beliefs. Looking back on the event, Dowell remarks, "Those words gave me the greatest relief that I have ever had in my life" (p. 46).

Dowell, unknown to himself, desires to live not in an adult world but in an illusory world. With the Ashburnhams he could transform reality into a pretty make-believe; he could rely on Leonora to shield him from unpleasantness. But the visit to M—— is not an unequivocal clue. Leonora, to be sure, shuts Dowell off from reality. Yet Edward is responsible for the very fact that Dowell evidently wants to escape, namely his wife's infidelity. Dowell has, and keeps, a particular need for Edward. The nature of this need becomes apparent only gradually, and deviously, since Dowell himself never fully understands it.

After he describes the visit to M——, Dowell continues with a seemingly random juxtaposition of events. Within a few pages in Chapter V, he alludes to the anxiety he used to feel over Florence's "heart"; he reveals that he never consummated his marriage because of Florence's illness; and into the midst of an account of Edward's arrest for kissing a nursemaid in a train, he suddenly interjects an accusation: "Is it possible that such a luckless devil [as Edward] should be so tormented by blind and inscrutable destiny? For there is no other way to think of it. None. I have the right to say it, since for years he was my wife's lover, since he killed her" (pp. 49-50). The accusation is astounding. So is Dowell's powerful expression of sympathy not for Florence but for Edward, for the man who loved his wife and "killed" her. Dowell explains neither his accusation nor his feelings. He proceeds with his account of Edward's amours.

The account reveals a noticeable bias. Indeed, Dowell virtually assumes the role of Edward's defender. He points out that, though Maisie Maidan, who really had a "heart," would have "succumbed to anything like a passionate embrace" (p. 54), Edward never made her his mistress. Leonora's treatment of "poor dear Edward's case" from the nursemaid onward amounted to "mismanagement" (p. 60). *Florence* was responsible for her affair with Edward, and Dowell hates her "with such a hatred that [he] would not spare her an eternity of loneliness" (p. 71). And he quotes Leonora's statement to Florence: "You murdered [Maisie]. You and I murdered her between us" (p. 72). Dowell concludes the first part of his narrative with the remark that Edward never felt much remorse over Maisie—and Edward's indifference is mirrored in Dowell himself.

By the end of Part One, Ford has revealed most of the important "facts" of *The Good Soldier,* and he has firmly directed our attention away from what has happened to why. From its deceptively calm opening paragraphs, the novel has transformed itself into a drama of sudden death and "murder." And the narrator who presented himself as a reliable witness has proved to be, comically, and perhaps tragically as well, a devotee of illusion. Dowell's failures in sensibility, his distortions of emphasis, his obvious bias for Edward, remain puzzling, almost exasperatingly so. But they are a thorough and subtle preparation for the psychological revelations that follow.

Toward the end of Part One, Dowell relates a vision of judgment that he has experienced:

> It is almost too terrible, the picture of that judgment, as it appears to me sometimes, at nights. It is probably the suggestion of some picture that I have seen somewhere. But upon an immense plain, suspended in midair, I seem to see three figures, two of them clasped close in an intense embrace, and one intolerably solitary. It is in black and white, my picture of that judgment, an etching, perhaps; only I cannot tell an etching from a photographic reproduction. And the immense plain is the hand of God, stretching out for miles and miles, with great spaces above it and below it. And they are in the sight of God, and it is Florence that is alone . . . (p. 70).

The figure of Florence "intolerably solitary" seems to be the creation of a guilty conscience. And almost immediately after he describes his vision, Dowell presents, in Part Two, an extended defense of his behavior toward his wife. But, unknown to himself, his presentation of his courtship and marriage is rich in ambiguities and disparities.

Dowell remarks that from the first moment he met Florence he "determined with all the obstinacy of a possibly weak nature, if not to make her mine, at least to marry her" (p. 78). The clause "if not to make her mine" carries the usual or expected meaning in such a context. A suitor may not gain possession of the woman he courts in the sense of winning her love, of making her his emotionally. But he may at least, if the woman is willing, marry her. There need not be, on this usual level, any implication that the marriage will not be consummated. On another level, however, that is precisely the implication. Marriage can be only a ceremony. Neither emotional nor physical possession is a necessary sequel to a wedding. Dowell apparently intends the conventional meaning, for he never admits that he did not want to consummate his marriage. Yet the second meaning receives considerable support elsewhere in the narrative.

Dowell goes on to say that he thinks his suit to Florence did not progress much at first, "perhaps" because he visited her in the daytime in the heat of summer, whereas "the night, I believe, is the proper season for the gentle feats of love, not a Connecticut July afternoon, when any sort of proximity is an almost appalling thought" (p. 79). Again Dowell seems to display a conventional attitude toward love and marriage. He assumes that lack of ardor is an obstacle to courtship. He excuses his by attributing it to the heat of a Connecticut July. But "perhaps" admits uncertainty and "I believe" implies that Dowell did not know the proper time even for the *gentle* feats of love. When Dowell continues with a list of Florence's "simple wants," a list that includes the item "she did not want much physical passion" (p. 79), the motive of his entire courtship becomes apparent. Explicitly, Dowell always presents his attraction to Florence as a mystery. "I just drifted in and wanted Florence" (p. 15). Unconsciously, however, he suggests that he wished to marry a woman who would make no emotional demands upon him, that he regarded Florence as such a woman.

Dowell received the first of a series of surprises from Florence in Waterbury, Connecticut. When he mounted a rope ladder and suddenly found himself in Florence's bedroom, she greeted him "with an embrace of a warmth" (p. 83). Dowell suggests that if he had also "shown warmth" at that moment, Florence would have been a "proper wife" to him. But he was in a hurry; he was afraid Florence's family would discover him; and he received her embrace, the first he had ever received from any woman, "with a certain amount of absence of mind." In short, he "was out of that room and down the ladder in under half a minute." Once more, Dowell blames himself for no emotional incapacity; he admits only to "a certain amount of absence of mind" induced by practical considerations. But the speed of his exit hints at stronger motives. Nor is a second excuse, which he adds to his first, entirely convincing: "I acted like a Philadelphia gentleman" (p. 83).

While he alludes to his own good manners, Dowell begins to discredit Florence. He thinks that his wife's delay in descending the ladder was the "only sign Florence ever showed of having a conscience as far as I was concerned." He even suggests that the initial warmth of her embrace may also have been just a "sign of conscience" (p. 83). In a similar way, he progressively distorts Florence's feelings for Jimmy, her first lover whom she met before her marriage and whom she rejoined in Paris afterwards.

Florence herself had told Leonora that she had an "overmastering passion" for Jimmy (p. 85). But Dowell transforms it into a milder emotion: "I suppose," he says, "she really cared for that imbecile" (p. 85). Then, after an extremely unflattering picture of Jimmy, Dowell dilutes Florence's feeling further still: "No, she cannot have liked that fellow long" (p. 88). Finally, he arrives at a complete contradiction of Florence's own statement to Leonora. "Her passion for Jimmy," he says, "was not even a passion" (p. 92). In Part One of the narrative, Dowell has already insisted on a similar interpretation of Florence's attachment to Edward. After his vision of judgment he says that Florence did not "need" to have an affair with Edward because she did not have the "hot passions" of Europeans (p. 71). The motive behind Dowell's distortions is clear enough. If Florence was not driven to her lovers by passion, if indeed she was a cold woman, then Dowell himself can hardly have failed her as a husband.

At the same time that he denies that Florence was in love with Jimmy, Dowell begins to offer assurances of his own masculinity. Florence had already announced before her marriage that she might have a bad heart like her Uncle Hurlbird's. Then "not ten minutes out from Sandy Hook [. . .] Florence went down into her cabin and her heart took her" (p. 86). This attack was, as Dowell explains, the only reason he never consummated his marriage. The ship's doctor advised him to "refrain from manifestations of affection" (p. 87).

With increasing self-confidence, Dowell compares himself to Jimmy and concludes: "Why, I was much the better man" (p. 87). And in the process of his self-aggrandizement he returns to an incident he has already described in order to offer a new interpretation. Florence used to give him an enigmatic smile at the door of the bathing place at Nauheim. He always wondered why she did it. Now he thinks he knows. That smile was a "sort of invitation" (p. 88). Having converted himself into a better man than Jimmy and an attractive husband to Florence, Dowell caps his claim to masculinity with an assertion of his physical strength. He insists that, wearisome as the task was, he did everything he could to preserve his ailing wife. In his devotion, in fact, he frightened Florence. On their way to the honeymoon ship *Pocohantas*, Dowell had entrusted a suitcase that supposedly contained Florence's heart remedies to his old Negro servant Julius. Julius, however, dropped his burden, to Dowell the "symbol of the existence of an adored wife of a day." At this misadventure, Dowell lost his temper. He punched Julius in the eye and threatened to strangle him. That act of anger, Dowell now reflects, had drastic consequences. It made Florence afraid of him—so much afraid that she dared not reveal to him her non-virginity. "For that," Dowell concludes, "was really the mainspring of her fantastic actions. She was afraid that I should murder her. . . . So she got up the heart attack, at the earliest possible opportunity, on board the liner" (pp. 92-93).

Dowell presents Florence first as a woman who embraced him with warmth; then as an opportunist who ruthlessly married him to rejoin Jimmy in Paris; finally as a woman terrified of "murder." He emerges from the explicit account of his marriage as a man far better than Jimmy—and a man of strength and impulsive temper. But his open defense of his manhood has been consistently belied by the ambiguities and progressive distortions in his narrative. Was it, after all, "refuge" from his disquieting vision of Florence "intolerably solitary" that Dowell sought with the Ashburnhams? Did they foster his illusion of manliness, as he himself tries to foster it? They did, in fact, just the reverse. Dowell remarks in Part One that Edward regarded him as a "woman or a solicitor" (p. 28), while Leonora looked at him as a mother looks at a son or as a sister looks at a brother or as "any kind woman may look at a poor chap in a bath chair" (p. 33). It was, Dowell complains, a "mortifying" experience. He must therefore have found another kind of security with the Ashburnhams. In the remainder of Part Two and in Chapter I, Part Three, Dowell so juxtaposes events and his responses to them that he unconsciously provides the final clues to his personality.

Dowell carries his account of his courtship and marriage to the point where Edward replaces Jimmy as Florence's lover. Then he repeats, in much stronger terms, the affection he displayed for

Edward in Part One: "Have I conveyed to you the splendid fellow that he was—the fine soldier, the excellent landlord, the extraordinarily kind, careful, and industrious magistrate, the upright, honest, fair-dealing, fair-thinking, public character?" (p. 93). He returns to his own marriage with a rapid account of Florence's death. Florence ran into the lounge at Nauheim "with a face whiter than paper"; Bagshawe exclaimed to Dowell, "By Jove! Florry Hurlbird. [. . .] The last time I saw that girl she was coming out of the bedroom of a young man called Jimmy at five o'clock in the morning"; and "a long time afterwards" Dowell went upstairs and did what he had never done since the night of his marriage—he entered Florence's bedroom. He found her lying dead, "quite respectably arranged, unlike Mrs. Maidan" (p. 102). He thought that Florence had had a heart attack.

Dowell follows this scene almost immediately with a fuller account of the conversation he had with Leonora on the afternoon he began writing his narrative. Bagshawe's remark about Florence and Jimmy was Dowell's first knowledge of that affair. The conversation with Leonora gave him the additional news that Florence and Edward were lovers and that Florence committed suicide. Dowell comments first, "I remember no emotion of any sort," then adds, "I cannot tell you the extraordinary sense of leisure that we two seemed to have at that moment. It wasn't as if we were waiting for a train, it wasn't as if we were waiting for a meal—it was just that there was nothing to wait for" (p. 105). And the scene with Leonora takes place in a comfortable interior, in Leonora's study, with twilight outside and the "remote and intermittent sound of the wind" (p. 105). It is a moment of peace, of relaxation, of security, a moment that contrasts with the "immense plain" of Dowell's vision of judgment, with the sense of "nakedness" he felt in the early years of his marriage, as if he were "on the sea-shore or in any great open space."

After this scene with Leonora, Dowell returns to Nauheim in the summer of 1913. He describes the growth of Edward's love, and of his own, for the girl Nancy Rufford. Far from displaying any jealousy, Dowell grows eloquent in praise of Edward's love for the girl he himself loves:

For every man there comes at last a time of life when the woman who then sets her seal upon his imagination has set her seal for good. He will travel over no more horizons; he will never again set the knapsack over his shoulders; he will retire from those scenes. He will have gone out of the business.

That at any rate was the case with Edward and the poor girl. It was quite literally the case. It was quite literally the case that his passions—for the mistress of the Grand Duke, for Mrs. Basil, for little Mrs. Maidan, for Florence, for whom you will—these passions were merely preliminary canters compared to his final race with death for her. [. . .] I don't mean to say that he didn't wear himself as thin as a lath in the endeavour to capture the other women; but over her he wore himself to rags and tatters and death—in the effort to leave her alone (pp. 115-116).

As the imagery suggests, Dowell views Edward's love for Nancy as a culmination, as a catharsis even. Yet it is not the usual happy resolution to a love story. Dowell rejoices in Edward's renunciation of Nancy.

Dowell returns, then, to Florence, and *this* time he explicitly exonerates Edward from responsibility for her death, even though Florence loved Edward, even though the moment before her suicide she had heard Edward avow his love for Nancy. "I am convinced," Dowell says, "that the sight of Mr. Bagshawe and the thought that Mr. Bagshawe . . . would almost certainly reveal to me that he had caught her coming out of Jimmy's bedroom at five o'clock in the morning on the 4th of August 1900—that was the determining influence in her suicide" (p. 119). Dowell finishes his account of August 4, 1913 with a complete description of his reactions at the time of his wife's death. He describes, once again, a moment of peace, relaxation, security. Like Maisie, Florence dies unattended by remorse.

Part Two and the first chapter of Part Three repeat in certain ways the sequence of Dowell's narrative in the closing chapters of Part One. After his account of the visit to M——, Dowell alludes to Florence's "heart" and to his extreme anxiety over it. He expresses profound pity for Edward as he accuses Edward of his wife's death. Then he notes that Edward never made Maisie his mistress; relates Maisie's death; and repeats Leonora's opinion to the effect that she and Florence, not Edward, were Maisie's "murderers." Immediately afterwards, Dowell refers again, and in much greater detail, to Florence's "heart" and to his own anxiety. Again too, he displays pity, and manifest affection as well, for Edward. Then he praises Edward's love for Nancy, a love that, again, Edward never consummated. Finally, he lays the blame for Florence's suicide on Bagshawe and Jimmy and so exonerates Edward. The parallel between the two sequences of events is not, to be sure, exact, since various of the figures in the drama change. But the general pattern is nonetheless constant: Dowell's anxiety over Florence, his allusion to Edward's unconsummated love, his disposition to free Edward from responsibility for "murder" and to lay the blame elsewhere.

The significance of this pattern hinges, finally, on Dowell's relationship with Edward. In Chapter I, Part Three, a fact that Dowell's profound pity for Edward in Part One has already intimated becomes abundantly clear. Dowell has identified with Edward, to the point where he has begun to live vicariously through him. His own love for Nancy was "unconscious" (p. 103); so was Edward's (p. 111). After Dowell spoke of his love, it became the major concern of his life (p. 121). Edward had the same experience (p. 116). And, of course, the order of the narration—Dowell surrounds his account of Edward's love for Nancy with references to his own love for the girl—underlines the identification.

"At what, then," to borrow a sentence of Dowell's, "does it all work out?" In the parallel narrative pattern, read "Dowell" for his alter ego "Edward." The pattern then becomes one of anxiety or guilt, denial or atonement, and exoneration. Dowell expresses his extreme worry over Florence, pities himself, assures his "silent listener" that he is capable of "innocent" or unconsummated love, and that he is, finally, not guilty of his wife's death.

Consider again Dowell's account of his marriage. His emotional responses to events are in every way exaggerated. After Florence embraced him, he was "out of that window and down the ladder in under half a minute." His precipitate exit suggests panic rather than, as he says, worry over relatives and the practical details of his elopement. The next day, although Florence had so far informed him only that she might have a "heart" like her Uncle Hurlbird's, Dowell regarded the suitcase that supposedly held her medicine as the very symbol of her existence; he struck Julius for dropping it and threatened to strangle him. Later in Paris, though Florence had actually simulated a heart attack, Dowell's anxiety continued to be extreme: "I seemed to see poor Florence die ten times a day—a little, pale, frail corpse" (p. 88). And he thought of entering her bedroom as a crime: "Why, I would as soon have thought of entering her room without her permission as of burgling a church. I would sooner have committed that crime" (pp. 88-89).

Dowell is, of course, a romantic hero; he prefers illusions to reality, and longs for an existence that is beautiful, proud, scrupulously decorous, and controlled. And he is an immature hero. Like Kelleg and like Grimshaw on the implicit level of *A Call*, he is sexually diffident. In *The Good Soldier*, indeed, Ford takes up and, with admirable psychological perception, carries to genuine completion his earlier themes of guilt and shame, love and violence. Dowell is not only incapable of sexual relationship with a woman; he is deeply afraid of it. His account of his courtship and marriage suggests that merely by entering Florence's room in Waterbury, merely by submitting to her embrace, he believes that he indulged in a shameful display of passion and that he thereby put Florence's life in jeopardy.

On the conscious level of his narrative, Dowell defends his masculinity and resents any slur against it. But in the first chapter of Part One he announces with considerable feeling: "I solemnly avow that not only have I never so much as hinted at an impropriety in my conversation in the whole of my days; and more than that, I will vouch for the cleanness of my thoughts and the absolute chastity of my life" (pp. 11-12). Unconsciously, he attempts to prove himself not a mature man but one who is *absolutely* chaste, whose feelings toward women are entirely innocent and childlike. It is that attempt that motivates his friendship with the Ashburnhams.

In Part One, Dowell interweaves his recital of his feud with the Belgian Railway, whose connections were so closely timed that Florence had to run to catch the Paris train, with an explanation of his affection for Leonora. The conjunction is significant:

> You see, in those days I was interested in people with "hearts."
> There was Florence, there was Edward Ashburnham—or, per-

haps, it was Leonora that I was more interested in. I don't mean in the way of love. But, you see, we were both of the same profession—at any rate as I saw it. And the profession was that of keeping heart patients alive (p. 47).

So Dowell thought that Leonora listened with sympathy to his plans for a "shock-proof world" (p. 49). He imagined that she believed, as he did, that "the whole world ought to be arranged so as to ensure the keeping alive of heart patients" (p. 47). In her he found a welcome confidante and an apparent aide-de-camp in his compulsive campaign to sustain Florence's life. When Leonora placed him, furthermore, in the immature or dependent roles of son, brother, or invalid, he received assurance of his absolute and childlike innocence.

Edward, of course, serves Dowell, first, as a scapegoat. *Edward* killed Florence. Then through Edward's unconsummated love for the "poor child" Maisie, who only "play[s]" at love (p. 51), Dowell again assures himself vicariously of his own innocence and enjoys the relief of a death for which he feels no remorse. As he turns to the events of August 4, 1913, Dowell once more uses Edward as a scapegoat. When he learns of Edward's affair with Florence, he suddenly feels relaxed and secure. He need not think that he has threatened Florence's life with his shameful emotional display. Edward was "more intimate" with Florence than he was himself (p. 107). Finally, through Edward, Dowell enjoys another experience of "innocent" love, with Nancy. And from Edward he now shifts the blame for his wife's death to Bagshawe and to Jimmy, who had made love to Florence long ago, before her marriage.

Dowell never understands himself. But as he fully describes his reactions to his wife's death, he unconsciously offers a symbolic expression of his relief from guilt:

> It was a feeling so tranquil. It was as if an immensely heavy— an unbearably heavy knapsack, supported upon my shoulders by straps, had fallen off and had left my shoulders themselves, that the straps had cut into, numb and without sensation of life. I tell you, I had no regret. What had I to regret? (p. 120).

And though he had been "in hell" when Florence ran for the Paris train (p. 49), the sight of Florence running in Nauheim roused him

to action only "a long time afterwards" (p. 102). At the moment
of Bagshawe's revelation, the tie that bound Dowell to Florence,
his compulsive need to sustain her life, was dissolved. For him,
Florence ceased to exist before she died. His detailed account of
his reactions continues:

> I suppose that my inner soul—my dual personality—had realized
> long before that Florence was a personality of paper—that she
> represented a real human being with a heart, with feelings, with
> sympathies, and with emotions only as a bank note represents
> a certain quantity of gold. I know that that sort of feeling
> came to the surface in me the moment the man Bagshawe told
> me that he had seen her coming out of that fellow's bedroom.
> I thought suddenly that she wasn't real; she was just a mass
> of talk out of guide-books, of drawings out of fashion-plates.
> It is even possible that if that feeling had not possessed me, I
> should have run up sooner to her room and might have pre-
> vented her drinking the prussic acid (pp. 120-121).

To reiterate for a moment, the chronological inversions and the
distortions of emphasis in *The Good Soldier* achieve verisimilitude.
They also provoke our active participation in the novel and force
us to recognize the complexity of truth. But Ford's "game" in *The
Good Soldier* is more "sinister" still. His narrative possesses, finally,
an organic psychological rhythm. Dowell's time shifts and his
unusual emphases are dictated by, and so reveal, the unconscious
motivations of his own personality.

As he describes his wife's death for the last time, Dowell remarks, "You have no idea how quite extraordinarily for me that
was the end of Florence. From that day to this I have never given
her another thought" (p. 120). His exaggeration strains our credulity; he remembers Florence only too well, and he has continued
to be ridden by his feelings of guilt and shame. In the involuted
course of his narrative, Dowell has lived through not one moment
of relaxation and quietude but three. And the mere succession of
these moments of catharsis implies that he must assure himself
again and again of his innocence. This suggestion is strengthened
by the nature of his feeling for Nancy, whom he claims that he
wants to marry (though, in the event, he never proposes to her).
He insists on her "entire innocence" (p. 123). He notes that she

possesses an "odd quality of sainthood" (p. 122). He even speaks of her in the very language he uses to describe his friendship with the Ashburnhams: "Why, she was like the sail of a ship, so white and definite in her movements" (p. 128). The peace of mind, then, that Dowell experiences in Part Three is only temporary. He still hopes to achieve a fully satisfactory resolution of his feelings of guilt.

III

Almost halfway through his narrative, Dowell remarks with characteristic naïveté: "I don't know that analysis of my own psychology matters at all to this story. I should say that it didn't or, at any rate, that I had given enough of it" (p. 103). But, as we have seen, Dowell's psychology has so far mattered most in *The Good Soldier*. He began his narrative with the apparent intention of telling a sad story about the Ashburnhams. He implied that the story was particularly sad because it called into question the whole nature of morality. Do people act morally, he asked, or do they only appear to do so? Soon, however, his distortions and contradictions showed that his chief concern was neither the Ashburnhams nor abstract morality but, simply, himself. He had to say that he had been lonely, Florence had deceived him, and, although he had made certain mistakes in his marriage, he was essentially innocent of its failure and of his wife's suicide.

Yet Dowell's vindication of himself, the story of his courtship and marriage, is only part of *The Good Soldier*. Dowell goes on to tell a second story, the one he began in the first place. After he finishes with Florence, Dowell turns his attention to Edward and Leonora Ashburnham. He has known them, of course, for years. Throughout the remainder of Part III, however, the emphasis of his narrative is not directly personal. His emotional involvement is noticeably less than it was in his account of his courtship and marriage. His questions are seldom urgent; he makes few accusations against his protagonists; he does not contradict himself without realizing it. In other words, as Dowell begins to recount the early histories of Edward and Leonora, his personality does not function as it functioned in the first half of the novel.

Ford has prepared for Dowell's detachment: there are at least two good reasons why Dowell may now stand away from his narrative. The less important is that he did not actually witness most of the events he now describes. He is primarily relaying information learned second-hand—from Edward and Leonora. A second and more important reason is that Dowell has already won his imaginative skirmish with Florence. He has asserted, to his own satisfaction, both his manliness and his innocence. Since the Ashburnham story does not, at least immediately, threaten his composure and he no longer needs to defend himself, he can afford the psychological luxury of objectivity. Dowell's new distance from his narrative, then, is plausible. Also, in juxtaposition with his previous involvement, it offers a further revelation of his moral character.

Dowell is so detached that he refuses to commit himself even to the facts of his story. Again and again, he avoids outright statement, habitually qualifying his narrative with such phrases as "it seems" or "it appears" and "I understand." In speaking of Leonora's love for Edward, for example, he says, "If his pulses never quickened she, so I have been told, became what is called an altered being when he approached her from the other side of a dancing floor" (pp. 140-141). And he is careful to set himself apart from the emotions experienced by the protagonists of his story. The amount of money Leonora's parents had to spend was "terrifying to them" (p. 138). Leonora's life after marriage was "almost heaven" for "a girl straight out of a convent" (p. 141).

Consistently Dowell's point of view is that he is conveying someone else's point of view. He divorces himself again and again from the entire social and moral milieu in which his story takes place. As an American, he does not really know the kind of life English army officers and their wives lead (p. 141). He does not know the geography of the Indian Empire (p. 172). Englishmen have always seemed to him "a little mad" in affairs of politics and religion (p. 147). Dowell, in fact, passes beyond detachment to the point of condescension. Leonora's father, he tells us, had "tenants on the brain" (p. 143) and a "bee in his bonnet" about agrarian economy (p. 144). Edward made Leonora "pretty speeches" (p. 140). He let her give "little treats" to her old friends, and she also enjoyed "chatterings" with other officers' wives (p. 141).

Dowell's criticism of his protagonists falls into a recognizable pattern. Leonora's inexperience with men is "almost impossible to imagine" (p. 135). Edward's purity of mind is an oddity "in this world" (p. 137). His belief that a man needs the cooperation of his wife in order to do his work well is "very simple" (p. 146). His affair with the Spanish dancer would not have been significant if he had not thought he owed her a measure of loyalty (p. 159). Why Major Basil, the husband of still another of Edward's mistresses, blackmailed Edward is difficult to understand—because the Major required the money for "no particular vices" (p. 165).

Dowell takes for granted, now, a cynical view of the world. People, he assumes, are motivated solely by personal gain of one variety or another. Those who deviate from this norm he judges neither good nor bad, merely simple or impractical. Indeed, Dowell deliberately denies any moral import to his story. He punctuates his narrative with such statements as "It is even very difficult to see how such things matter" (p. 151), and he finds what happens part of the "peculiar irony of things" (p. 149).

Although Dowell for the most part ignores his own experiences while he "talks" about the Ashburnhams, he does turn away from Edward and Leonora to discuss, twice and at some length, a trip he made to America after Florence's death. These digressions occupy their respective positions, in Chapter IV, Part Three, and in Chapter II, Part Four, partly to give the illusion of time passing. Dowell does not relate every step of the Ashburnham story in detail, and both digressions mark chronological gaps or compressions in his narrative. After each, he picks up his story at a stage more advanced than that at which he left it to describe psychological changes that have occurred in Edward and Leonora, changes that took time to happen.

The digressions therefore give the effect of verisimilitude. More importantly, they contribute to the novel's meaning, for each underlines Dowell's failure to make moral judgments. The point of the first digression, an anecdote about a Vermonter who was attended darkly by gossip just because he was a Democrat, is that it is extremely difficult to form a correct estimate of anyone's character. Dowell himself has, however, found a way to circumvent this difficulty: he has simply given up trying to judge character. As he puts it, "In my present frame of mind, nothing would ever make me make inquiries as to the character of any man that I liked at first sight. [. . .] For who in this world can give anyone a character? Who in this world knows anything of any other heart— or of his own?" (p. 155) The second digression shows Dowell making a similar "solution" to a similar problem. On his trip home, he visited Florence's aunts, the Misses Hurlbird, and unwittingly walked straight into a "moral dilemma" (p. 197). The question was whether Uncle Hurlbird's testamentary request for a heart memorial in his name should or should not be carried out. Miss Florence thought a lung memorial should be built instead, since Uncle Hurlbird had really died of lung trouble. Miss Emily thought no memorial at all should perpetuate the family name, because Florence had behaved so badly with Edward Ashburnham. Dowell's answer to the problem was, in effect, no answer at all: "I simply told my attorney that there was the million and a half; that he could invest it as he liked, and that the purposes must be decided by the Misses Hurlbird" (p. 200). The second digression not only under-lines Dowell's detachment; it virtually constitutes a parody of his evasion of moral issues.

Again, our point of view transcends Dowell's, whose attitude toward the Ashburnhams is patently inadequate. His narrative of love and hate does matter, and his facts have ethical import. His objectivity is therefore not a sign of maturity or of wisdom won from experience. On the contrary, Dowell has achieved peace of mind at the expense of conscience, and his cynicism really repre-sents another effort to escape reality.[7]

A further judgment of his narrator is not, however, all that Ford achieves by joining the account of Dowell's courtship and marriage with the early lives of Edward and Leonora. At first, it may seem that Ford has struck only random sparks of social satire from the Ashburnham story. Yet its bright comic surface composes a coherent

---

7. While our point of view always transcends Dowell's, it is interesting to note that he nonetheless sets the prevailing tone of his narrative. There is a decided, and comic, letdown in intensity after Florence's death. Then the novel begins to build toward a second and final climax.

pattern of judgment. As in *A Call*, Ford directs his criticism beyond his characters to the society they represent.

Ford's social comment appears not in spite of Dowell's detachment, but because of it. In his willingness to give someone else's point of view, Dowell explains the protagonists' motives and details their reactions to various events. Sometimes he even reproduces in indirect discourse their habitual thinking processes and ways of speaking. The result is that the other characters reveal themselves just as Dowell has. And as Dowell remarks that this or that does not matter or is merely a trick of destiny, we are doubly pressed to draw our own conclusions.

Dowell's amusing account of Edward's marriage to Leonora forms a consistent attack on certain attitudes toward relationships between men and women. Both Leonora's parents and Edward's show a manifest disregard for love and a distaste for passion, and both have rigorously raised their children to be "pure."

Leonora, whose youth is presented as a near-parody of a fairy tale, lived in a convent until, at the age of eighteen, she joined her parents in an isolated manor house that was "almost more cloistral" (p. 135) than the convent. Her sole companions were her mother, her father, and her six sisters:

> Only three times in the year that succeeded her coming home from the convent did she enter another person's house. For the rest of the time the seven sisters ran about in the neglected gardens between the unpruned espaliers. Or they played lawn-tennis or fives in an angle of a great wall that surrounded the garden—an angle from which the fruit trees had long died away. They painted in water-colour; they embroidered; they copied verses into albums (p. 135).

Because of her isolation, Leonora knew nothing about men. When Colonel Powys wrote to his old friend Colonel Ashburnham suggesting a marriage between one of his seven daughters and Edward Ashburnham, he boasted that all his girls were "tall, upstanding, clean-limbed, and absolutely pure" (p. 136). All his girls, that is, were absolutely ignorant of the facts of life and so ideally prepared for marriage.

The Ashburnhams, for their part, had brought up Edward to

be "almost as pure in mind as Leonora" (p. 137). Just before Colonel Powys's letter arrived, however, Edward had, in a "reflex action" (p. 137) that we recognize as humorously prophetic, looked twice at a pretty girl in the street. His mother was much alarmed. She was quite ready to welcome the suggestion that her son marry a Powys girl, because they were "so clean-run and so safe" (p. 139). After a formal visit, during which Edward satisfied everyone by finding the seven sisters so clean-run that he "regarded them rather as boys than as girls" (p. 139), Edward and Leonora were married.

Dowell finishes his account with the information that neither Edward nor Leonora knew until a few years after their marriage "how children are produced" (p. 147), and comments, in a masterpiece of understatement, "I dare say it had a good deal of influence on their mentalities" (p. 147). The sheer facts of the narrative prompt us to go beyond his tentative judgment. Both the Powyses and the Ashburnhams have, with a comical intensity of effort, cultivated emotional immaturity in their children and married them on the basis of social convenience. They are in part responsible for the unhappiness that waits for Edward and Leonora.

Like their parents, or perhaps because of their parents, both Edward and Leonora adopted unrealistic theories about men and women. Although the theories conflicted with each other with the comic symmetry of direct opposites, they were fundamentally similar. Each represented its believer's attempt to deny his or her own emotions. Edward drew from a number of novels the notion of a "pure and constant love" (p. 186). He thought that ties between men and women should be wholly spiritual in nature: women should be virtuous and tender and should give moral support to men, who, in return, should pledge to women their undying devotion and lifelong protection. Leonora did not read novels; she could not "stand" novels (p. 179). But she was instructed by her spiritual advisers, and took from them the notion that love was merely an animalistic activity indulged in by men and not by women, at least not by "nice" women:

> She saw life as a perpetual sex-battle between husbands who desire to be unfaithful to their wives, and wives who desire to recapture their husbands in the end. [. . .] Man, for her, was

a sort of brute who must have his divagations, his moments of excess, his nights out, his, let us say, rutting seasons (p. 186).

In practice, of course, neither theory proved reliable, although Edward and Leonora continued to hold each to his own. Edward thought he was looking for his ideal woman. But a number of turns in the narrative emphasize that, while his attraction to women may have been spiritual, it was always physical as well. The most conclusive arguments are the sheer number of his attachments— the nursemaid, the Spanish dancer, Mrs. Basil, Maisie Maidan, Florence, and Nancy—and their relatively brief duration. Before Maisie died, he had begun his flirtation with Florence. Before Florence drank poison, he had already realized that he loved Nancy. But Edward never really faced the implications of his experiences. He hoped that his feeling for the nursemaid in the train was "quite half-fatherly" (p. 150). His affair with the Spanish dancer he "sized up as a short attack of madness like hydrophobia" (p. 173), while Mrs. Basil was his "soul-mate" (p. 173). Except for an uneasy moment when his love for Maisie caused him to "suspect that he was inconstant" (p. 173), he clung to the notion that he was as pure and as faithful as the heroes of his novels.

Leonora's theory of love was just as unrealistic as Edward's. It led her, for example, to exaggerate to comic proportions the strength of Edward's sexual drive. At one period in her life, she entertained "the 'monstrous' theory" of Edward (p. 179). She thought that he tried to seduce every woman in sight. Later she modified her theory; she then thought that Edward needed to seduce only certain "types" of women (p. 181) and that he would necessarily arrive one day at her type. Leonora's own feelings contradicted her theory of women in love, for she was strongly attracted to Edward. But she never allowed herself to express her feelings or show them. By the exercise of considerable will power, she managed to simulate coldness to Edward throughout their married life.

As Dowell says, the differences between Edward and Leonora were "profound" (p. 147) and their marriage was an unbroken series of misunderstandings, a veritable tragicomedy of errors. And Ford has not limited the Ashburnham story to the private lives of Edward and Leonora. He also treats their public relationships, making them follow behavioral patterns that are, on a superficial level, diametrically opposed. Edward's generosity was "fantastic" (p. 141). He wanted to take on his shoulders responsibility for his tenants, his troop, his whole county. Leonora, on the other hand, disapproved of generosity and ran Edward's estate, Branshaw Teleragh, on strictly commercial principles. She dismissed her tenants when they failed to make a profit from their farms and disposed of family heirlooms as if they were so many shares of common stock. She did not want Edward to fight for his country, because she had heard that active duty was very expensive. Her only loyalties were personal or religious—she felt responsible for Edward, for Nancy, for Dowell, and to a certain extent for Maisie Maidan, because she and Maisie came from the same convent. She was, also, scrupulously faithful to the duties imposed on her by the Roman Catholic Church.

Dowell tries to account for these conflicting social attitudes and actions by pointing out that Edward and Leonora were brought up in different traditions, one collective, the other individualistic. His explanation is not wrong—it is simply incomplete. Edward did, for instance, sympathize with the poor and the unfortunate. He was indeed the good soldier, the good landlord, the "father of his people" (p. 167). But at the same time, like Katharine Howard and the young Lovell, Edward sought to fulfill a romantic conception of himself. He was also the man who liked to engage in endless discussions of his ideals and solicit admiration for them. "He found ... quite a number of ladies in his set who were capable of agreeing with this handsome and fine fellow that the duties of a feudal gentleman were feudal" (p. 158). He even sought admiration from the Spanish dancer. In return for La Dolciquita's sacrifice of her "virtue," he would cherish her for life. And "in return, again, for his honourable love she would listen forever to the accounts of his estate" (p. 161). When La Dolciquita declined this reciprocal arrangement, Edward for the moment replaced his feudal role with another romantic pose. He adopted "an attitude of Byronic gloom—as if his court had gone into half-mourning" (p. 164).

Leonora had been "drilled [. . .] to keep her mouth shut" (p. 177). She did not discuss her ideals. But she, too, tried to achieve a romantic standard of conduct. She thrust gifts upon Edward because she wanted to do the "threadbare business" (p. 168), to play the role of the devoted and self-sacrificing wife. She regarded her efficient management of Branshaw as so many "good deeds" (p. 179). Even her longing for Edward's love sprang in part from her wish to fulfill a virtuous conception of herself. "She would show, in fact, that in an unfaithful world one Catholic woman had succeeded in retaining the fidelity of her husband" (p. 187).

If Edward and Leonora were, as Dowell says, "two noble people" (p. 164), the very splendor of their ideals betrays the fact that they were also egoistic. Each of them chose a code of conduct that demanded punctilious self-control, even self-abnegation. Edward would be a pure and constant lover, a thoroughgoing altruist. Leonora espoused, not Edward, but an almost conventual rule of religious and domestic duty.

At this point, the relationship between Dowell's first story and his second becomes clear. Dowell and Edward and Leonora exemplify three attitudes toward experience that are superficially different but basically similar. Each attitude represents an attempt to escape from reality, to escape, particularly, from a frank recognition of human nature. Dowell, who is afraid of feeling, has literally run from intimacy with Florence. Edward, who has also refused to adjust to the fact of passion, has consistently tried to romanticize his feelings for women. Leonora has relegated sex to men only. These attitudes are echoed in one form or another by the minor characters in the novel—by the Ashburnhams who arranged a "safe" marriage, by the nuns who counseled Leonora, by the Misses Hurlbird who could not bring themselves to warn Dowell of Florence's affair with Jimmy, and by Uncle Hurlbird who concluded his nuptial "lecture" to Dowell with the "aspiration that all American women should one day be sexless" (p. 86).

The Ashburnham story therefore develops the theme inherent in the story of Dowell's courtship and marriage. It shows that, despite his idiosyncrasies, Dowell is not a special case. He may be sexually diffident; he may be incapable of passion; but, for their part, Edward and Leonora have pretended that they were, too. Edward and Leonora sought, besides, to fulfill overambitious public ideals of altruism and duty. Dowell and the Ashburnhams have all three lived in an illusory world, which has its own beauty but is false at its foundation. Ford has, then, continually deepened and illuminated the questions that Dowell voiced at the beginning of the novel. The discrepancy between society's standards of virtue and its behavior is not a simple matter of hypocrisy. People do not set up arbitrary rules and then deliberately break them, as Dowell suggested at the beginning of the novel. The standards which they cannot keep express—and this is the central paradox of the novel—some of their most profound aspirations. They represent no less than an attempt to make over human nature. That attempt, the novel suggests, is bound to fail because human beings are necessarily emotional and self-assertive and no amount of carefully constructed wishful thinking can make them otherwise.

The novel's attitude toward romantic idealism is reflected in the prevailing patterns of imagery. The images that appear most frequently are kinetic and may be termed images of endurance and of collapse. Since each category is used ambiguously, each supports the central paradox. Acting, playing the game, and setting the knapsack on one's shoulders are splendid, brave activities. So are pretending one has no feelings or personal aims and, even though one does, carrying on the conventions, the game, as if one doesn't. On the other hand, not acting, not playing the game, not setting the knapsack on one's shoulders—some words for these opposite activities are slackening, crashing, smashing, breaking, deteriorating—are rather unattractive activities, even though they spring from a recognition of truth.[8]

The Good Soldier suggests, furthermore, that there is a necessary connection between private morality and morality in general. The connection was introduced, first of all, by Dowell when he asked:

---

8. Other kinetic images, of relaxation or resolution, tantalizingly prophesy that there will be an end to enduring, a moment of catharsis, when one does achieve the innocence to which one aspires. Then the race is won, the journey is over, the knapsack slips from the shoulders. Complications are smoothed out, and one reaches one's dream city, Carcassonne. But there is an everlasting check to these hopes. The catharsis is never achieved on earth. Death is the only relaxation, the only rest, the only possible *nunc dimittis* from the otherwise unrespited game.

"If everything is so nebulous about a matter so elementary as the morals of sex, what is there to guide us in the more subtle morality of all other personal contacts, associations, and activities?" (p. 12) Later, Leonora voiced a series of rhetorical questions that are recognizably biased, but that nonetheless assume, and serve to recall, the same fundamental relationship between private morality and public. When she first realized in the castle at M—— that Edward and Florence had begun a flirtation, she hurried Dowell outside and turned upon him:

> "Don't you see?" she said, "don't you see what's going on?" [. . .]
> "Don't you see," she said, with a really horrible bitterness, with a really horrible lamentation in her voice, "Don't you see that that's the cause of the whole miserable affair; of the whole sorrow of the world? And of the eternal damnation of you and me and them . . ." (p. 45).

In context, it is clear that "what's going on" signifies the flirtation she has just witnessed between Edward and Florence. So does "that" in "that's the cause," while "the miserable affair" refers to the Protestant schism from the Roman Catholic faith. For Leonora thought that the real reason for the incidence and spread of Protestantism was the sexual desires of the men who promoted it. Sexual misbehavior is, in her view, the cause "of the whole sorrow of the world" and of everyone's "eternal damnation."

Leonora is extravagant, and her words are melodramatic. Yet a causal relationship not unlike the one she draws is illustrated by the novel as a whole. Dowell, who has failed to participate in any intimate relationship and has therefore, as it were, taken refuge in private amorality, has also declined the responsibility of any "more subtle morality." He is the man whose occupation was always "nothing." As he himself said, "I suppose I ought to have done something, but I didn't see any call to do it. Why does one do things?" (p. 15).

Hugh Kenner has claimed that Ford makes no definite commitments in *The Good Soldier*.[9] If we try to formulate, say, Ford's

---

9. "Conrad and Ford," *Shenandoah*, III (Summer, 1952), 50-55. This essay was reprinted in *Gnomon: Essays on Contemporary Literature* (New York, 1958).

opinions on the American character or on the Roman Catholic Church, we may be forced to agree. We are everywhere faced with ambiguities rather than certainties. But if we look for some more general truth, we can see that Ford certainly has committed himself. He has clearly implied that public and private morality are intimately related, and that there can be no true morality unless society's standards of conduct are built on a realistic view of human nature. These ideas constitute the positive values of *The Good Soldier* and they are, I think, values that deserve agreement.

IV

After the account of the Ashburnham marriage, *The Good Soldier* focuses for a time on Nancy Rufford. With his treatment of Nancy, Ford presents still another variation on his theme of romantic idealism; in certain respects, it is almost as if he begins to rewrite his novel in Part Four. He has endowed Nancy with Dowell's most striking initial quality, naïveté. Just as Dowell once did, Nancy believes in appearances. She feels quite secure in her life at Branshaw. She not only thinks that Edward and Leonora are a "model couple" but thinks that all marriages, at least between people she knows, are based on love—and her notion of love excludes passion. Again like Dowell, Nancy is bound for disillusion. The discrepancy between her view of the world and the world as it really is constitutes a potential source of shock and unhappiness.

The first step in Nancy's awakening is her realization that Edward is "a man with his ups and downs and not an invariably gay uncle like a nice dog, a trustworthy horse, or a girl friend" (p. 207). Further observation brings home to her the fact that Edward does not love Leonora and that Leonora hates him. Then, in the newspapers, she makes a still more disquieting discovery. She reads an account of a divorce granted to Mr. and Mrs. Brand, whom she knows. To her, it seems a "queer affair" (p. 218). She thinks it strange that one of the counsel at the trial cross-questioned Mr. Brand about his feelings for Miss Lupton, a third acquaintance of hers. Then, reading on, she learns that Mr. Brand has committed adultery with Miss Lupton. "[The] words conveyed nothing to Nancy—nothing real, that is to say. She knew that one was commanded not to commit adultery—but, why, she thought, should one? It was probably something like catching salmon out of season—a thing one did not do" (p. 219). When Nancy questions Leonora about the case, Leonora informs her bluntly that the divorce means that Mr. Brand can now marry Miss Lupton. Nancy is terrified. It occurs to her that Edward might be in love with someone else and that he, too, might marry again.

Then Nancy makes her most shocking discovery about human nature:

> One evening she went into Edward's gunroom—he had gone to a meeting of the National Reserve Committee. On the table beside his chair was a decanter of whiskey. She poured out a wine-glassful and drank it off.
>
> Flame then really seemed to fill her body; her legs swelled; her face grew feverish. She dragged her tall height up to her room and lay in the dark. The bed reeled beneath her; she gave way to the thought that she was in Edward's arms; that he was kissing her on her face, that burned; on her shoulders, that burned, and on her neck, that was on fire (p. 225).

Nancy realizes that she loves Edward and that her love is passionate. Not only Mr. Brand and Miss Lupton and Edward are capable of transgressing the moral standards of "good people"— she herself is capable of it.

The incident recalls Dowell's confrontation of Florence in Waterbury, Connecticut. Nancy cannot endure Edward's imagined embrace any more than Dowell could endure Florence's real one. Her thoughts "died out of her mind; they left only a feeling of shame so insupportable that her brain could not take it in and they vanished." She atones for her offense by deciding to live as a saint, a "personage with a depressed, earnest face and tightly closed lips, in a clear white room, watering flowers or tending an embroidery frame," and by desiring "to go with Edward to Africa and to throw herself in the path of a charging lion so that Edward might be saved for Leonora at the cost of her life" (pp. 225-226).

Nancy's participation in the ordinary human community is imputed to her a second time when her mother, who has not only deceived her father but probably worked as a prostitute, writes to her, "You ought to be on the streets with me. How do you know that you are even Colonel Rufford's daughter?" (p. 226). Again, Nancy responds with acts of denial and atonement. Resolving to "rescue" her mother (p. 229), she takes off her clothes, folds them neatly, and dresses herself in white.

Like Dowell, like Edward and Leonora, Nancy rejects things as they are. She believes that her mother's past can be effaced; she represses her own emotions; she transforms her love for Edward into a wholly spiritual experience. Nancy's ideal of love, in fact, is very similar to Edward's. She imagines herself giving to Edward the moral support he always claimed he wanted from women: "He must be sheltered by his love for her and by her love—her love from a great distance and unspoken, enveloping him, surrounding him, upholding him" (p. 229).

Ford's satire aims, as usual, at both the individual and society. It serves to criticize "good people" who cannot conform to their own code of conduct and who hide from their transgressions in an illusory world of innocence. It also criticizes Nancy for her self-deception and romantic, adolescent idealism. And yet, Ford's treatment of Nancy is also markedly kind, much more so than his treatment of Dowell or even of Edward or Leonora. While Nancy deceives herself, the reality that reaches her through a scandalous divorce case, through Leonora's hatred, and, finally, through her mother's cruelty is, after all, the reverse of engaging. Both Nancy's youth and the severity of her shocks are very much in her favor. On his youngest heroine, Ford's judgment lies very lightly.

While he discusses Nancy, Dowell's relationship to his narrative undergoes still another change. He does not understand himself, but, ironically, he does understand the schoolgirl who is so much like him. When, for example, he reports that Nancy told Leonora, "I am going to Glasgow—to take my mother away from there," Dowell comments: "She added: 'To the ends of the earth,' for, if the last months had made her nature that of a woman, her phrases were still romantically those of a school-girl" (p. 216). Here Dowell is actually pointing out humorous incongruities. He is informing us, sympathetically, that Nancy's use of language is inappropriate to her subject. While he speaks of Nancy, his attitude is, for the only extended period of the novel, virtually the same as ours.

Nancy's story is thus much more than a "rewriting." Her experience repeats key elements in Dowell's experience, in Edward's, in Leonora's, and it repeats them on a much more sympathetic level. In so submitting his theme to the strain not only of humor but also of compassion, Ford at once heightens its significance for us and increases the intensity of our reading experience.

v

With the beginning of the last two chapters of the novel, Ford subjects us once again to the full force of Dowell's personality. His attitude toward his story, it becomes immediately apparent, has undergone a final significant change. He has lost all trace of the detachment he reached after his account of his courtship and marriage and displays instead a strong emotional reaction to the events he relates. His dominant feelings are anger, bitterness, self-pity.

The reasons for the change are obvious. During the eighteen-month interval that separates these chapters from the previous narration, crucial changes have occurred in the lives of all three survivors in the story. Nancy was sent out to her father in Ceylon. She read of Edward's suicide when her boat stopped at Aden; in the Red Sea she went mad. At Leonora's request, Dowell has fetched the girl home to Branshaw and assumed permanent responsibility for her. While he was gone, Leonora left Branshaw to marry an old suitor, Rodney Bayham. She expects to bear him a child in a few months.[10]

---

10. Ford clearly intended to withhold these events until the end of his novel, for he carefully makes Dowell note the time when he learned of Nancy's madness: Leonora brought him the news at the moment in the narrative marked by the end of Chapter IV, Part Four. But Ford has slipped up factually, since Dowell has alluded to Nancy's fate at several prior points (on pages 28, 69, 121, and 206).

These allusions indicate that Ford worked out the precise nature of Nancy's fate only after he started writing and that he intended originally to give Dowell full knowledge of her fate from the beginning. Later he must have seen the artistic advantages of withholding the news not only of Leonora's marriage, but of Nancy's madness as well. These eleventh-hour revelations are vital to Dowell's psychology. Together with the final change they cause in his point of view, they form the climax of the novel.

All these events contribute to the ironic frustration of Dowell's aspirations toward innocence. Nancy is not his wife, but his dependent. His relationship with her does not provide the sort of heaven he wanted, but a reminder of the hell he experienced with Florence: he must act, as long as he lives, the role of "nurse-attendant" (p. 237), just as he acted it for thirteen years with Florence. And Leonora, who used to provide him with the illusion of a world innocent of sex, has entered into a sexual relationship. Dowell's attitude, then, is an aggrieved expression of futility and defeat. He voices the old complaints of his life with Florence. He is just as lonely, as isolated, and as tired as he was before he met the Ashburnhams.

Who is to blame? At one point, an unaccommodating universe, at another, society, and then, in turn, Edward, Nancy, and Leonora. Dowell's accusations do not form a coherent pattern, and he contradicts himself from one moment to the next. From the welter of criticism, however, various judgments emerge that betray his continued preference for illusion. He shows sympathy for Edward's and Nancy's sentimental desire to go on loving each other from a distance of 5000 miles. They seem to him "splendid creatures" (p. 239), the only people he ever loved. Much earlier, in Part One, he remarked that he "loved Leonora always," but, now, he is predictably malicious about her marriage: "Leonora survives, the perfectly normal type, married to a man who is rather like a rabbit. For Rodney Bayham is rather like a rabbit and I hear that Leonora is expected to have a baby in three months' time" (pp. 238-239).

Throughout the narrative, Dowell remains unaware of his own nature. He implies more than once that his love for Nancy was passionate. His strongest assertion of masculinity, however, appears to be his identification with Edward, which becomes explicit in this section of the narrative:

I can't conceal from myself the fact that I loved Edward Ashburnham—and that I love him because he was just myself. If I had had the courage and the virility and possibly also the physique of Edward Ashburnham I should, I fancy, have done much what he did (p. 253).

The passage has many implications. If superficially the comparison is fatuous, as Schorer has remarked, on another level it is valid, since Edward and Dowell both sought absolute innocence. The passage therefore becomes deeply ironic. Dowell's identification with Edward is not, as he implies, a proof of his masculinity, but of his unconscious desire to assert his emotional immaturity.

Early in the novel, Dowell indicated that the problems raised by the story he had to tell might "work out" (p. 12). At the end of his narration, he admits that he has not been able to "work out" anything after all. His thoughts travel endlessly "round and round" a circular course that yields no meaning (p. 233). He therefore resigns himself, plaintively and childishly, to ignorance:

> Well, it is all over. Not one of us has got what he really wanted. Leonora wanted Edward, and she has got Rodney Bayham, a pleasant enough sort of sheep. Florence wanted Branshaw, and it is I who have bought it from Leonora. I didn't really want it; what I wanted mostly was to cease being a nurse-attendant. Well, I am a nurse-attendant. Edward wanted Nancy Rufford and I have got her. Only she is mad. It is a queer and fantastic world. Why can't people have what they want? The things were all there to content everybody; yet everybody has the wrong thing. Perhaps you can make head or tail of it; it is beyond me (p. 237).

But Ford has implied, of course, a meaning in the story that Dowell cannot, or perhaps will not, find. The tragicomic destinies of Edward, Nancy, Leonora, and Dowell are the final result of their persistent flight from reality. They are all responsible for their "broken, tumultuous, agonized, and unromantic lives" (p. 238).

In one of his many discussions on the form of the novel, Ford wrote:

> The whole novel [should] be an exhaustion of aspects, [should] proceed to one culmination, to reveal once and for all, in the last sentence, or the penultimate; in the last phrase, or the one before it—the psychological significance of the whole. (Of course, you might have what is called in music your coda.)[11]

---

11. Ford Madox Hueffer, *Thus to Revisit: Some Reminiscences* (London: Chapman & Hall, 1921), p. 44.

With this statement as a guide to his intentions, there seems little doubt that Ford placed at the end of *The Good Soldier* not only climactic ultimate and penultimate sentences, but an actual coda— an entire final passage that brings the book to a definite and formal close, revealing "once and for all" its significance.

On the first page of the novel, Dowell reveals that Edward Ashburnham is already dead; in the second half of the novel he adds incidentally to this information the fact that Edward committed suicide by cutting his throat. But it is only at the very end of his narrative, after he has told everything else, that Dowell remarks ingenuously, "It suddenly occurs to me that I have forgotten to say how Edward met his death" (p. 255).

The account, which covers less than two pages, re-creates the novel's total attitude toward romantic idealism. It is, first of all, moving; for Edward did kill himself for love, and he resolved to do it with exquisite nonchalance. At the same time, the suicide has its comic aspects. To begin with, Edward was too handsome, rather like a caricature than a portrait: "He was quite sober, quite quiet, his skin was clear-coloured; his hair was golden and perfectly brushed; the level brick-dust red of his complexion went clean up to the rims of his eyelids; his eyes were porcelain blue" (p. 255). And he was playing the English gentleman to more than perfection. He was inspecting his stables and talking about "the necessity of getting the numbers of the Hampshire territorials up to the proper standard." Then he opened a telegram from Nancy "negligently." Its message—"Safe Brindisi. Having rattling good time"—he read "without emotion." He said to Dowell, "You might just take that wire to Leonora." The easygoing slang and pronounced understatement of his final remark—"So long, old man, I must have a bit of a rest, you know"—pass the limits of tight-lipped heroism and slide into parody. As Dowell comments, Edward was "to the last, a sentimentalist, whose mind was composed of indifferent poems and novels."

And Edward was not the only actor in this final scene who kept a stiff upper lip. Nancy's telegram, composed in schoolgirl slang was ostentatiously cheerful. Leonora's reaction to it was also cheerful, as well as conventional. She was "quite pleased" when she read the message. For his part, Dowell did nothing to mar the total performance. In effect, he sanctioned it. When he "trotted off with the telegram to Leonora," he made no mention of Edward's determination to commit suicide. He merely comments later that he would have liked to say, "God bless you" to Edward. But he did not do so. He thought that such a remark would not be "quite English good form."

With its combination of sympathy and satire the coda seems to present Ford's judgment of his original version of the Ashburnham story in *The Spirit of the People*. There he sums up, in reference not to the suicide, which occurs only in *The Good Soldier*, but to the parting at the station:

> Now, in its particular way this was a very fine achievement; it was playing the game to the bitter end. [. . .] It may have been desirable, in the face of the eternal verities—the verities that bind together all nations and all creeds—that the parting should have been complete and decently arranged. But a silence so utter, a so demonstrative lack of tenderness, seems to me to be a manifestation of a national characteristic that is almost appalling.[12]

In the coda, however, Ford has passed far beyond his original judgment. He still scores the English disregard for feeling. But he also epitomizes the profound motives that create and maintain his given social tradition. For every detail of the coda implies that Edward, Nancy, Leonora, and Dowell were not merely adhering to an arbitrary code of behavior. Under the guise of "playing the game," each of them was expressing his own desires.

By cutting his throat, Edward punished himself for his failure to achieve his own ideals. Nancy's telegram not only crowned her rejection of Edward's love but served as a forcible reminder of the passionate nature of that love. Edward could not, while he lived, be "pure," as his code of conduct demanded. He could condemn his impurity. The laconic manner of his suicide, which precluded any expression of sympathy (he looked at Dowell with a

---

12. Ford Madox Hueffer, *The Spirit of the People: An Analysis of the English Mind* (London: Alston Rivers, 1907), pp. 150-151. Also published in *England and the English: An Interpretation* (New York: McClure, Phillips, 1907).

"direct, challenging, brow-beating glare"), emphasizes its self-accusing nature.

The actions of Nancy and Leonora also exemplify a rejection of passion. Under Leonora's influence, Nancy finally ceased to idealize Edward and transform her love for him into a spiritual attachment. Instead, she regarded Edward as a brute and mercilessly castigated him for his sexual impulses. Her telegram, with its careless slang, was a deliberate action of cruelty. Leonora, of course, sanctioned Nancy's cruelty, and it is even possible that she sanctioned Edward's suicide. On one of his last evenings at Branshaw she had thought that Edward was going to kill himself. Although she happened to be wrong—he was merely cleaning his gun—the instance shows that she suspected Edward's tendency toward self-destruction. But when the telegram came, she did nothing and was "quite pleased."

By his own admission, Dowell virtually gave Edward his permission to commit suicide:

> Why should I hinder him?
> I didn't think he was wanted in the world, let his confounded tenants, his rifle-associations, his drunkards, reclaimed and unreclaimed, get on as they liked. Not all the hundreds and hundreds of them deserved that that poor devil should go on suffering for their sakes.

Dowell sanctioned the suicide, not because he regarded Edward as a brute, but because he regarded him as just the reverse. Influenced by the apparently "pure" character of Edward's love for Nancy, Dowell came to accept Edward as a man innocent of passion. He identified with Edward and converted him finally into a symbol of his own frustrations and grievances at the hands of women in particular and the world in general. Through Edward's suicide, Dowell was able to appropriate to himself all the pleasures of martyrdom without any of its woes. Thus the coda reveals, as Ford declared it should, the "psychological significance of the whole."

Ford revealed his theme even more succinctly elsewhere. Underneath the title *The Good Soldier: A Tale of Passion*, he placed as epigraph the phrase *Beati Immaculati*. Applied to the novel, these words from the Vulgate version of the one hundred and eighteenth Psalm are plainly ironic; and, in choosing them, Ford has indicated the controlling design of his novel. His protagonists all refused to face the fact of their own human nature but pursued instead an impossible standard of innocence. It was precisely because they tried too far to walk in the way of honor that they were neither blessed nor stainless.

The Good Soldier rests, I think, on a severe and wonderful achievement of self-criticism. If Ford's own psychic needs seem to contribute to the relatively indifferent quality of his apprentice work, they determine in part his good fiction as well. His preoccupation with guilt and shame, with the longing for innocence and the need for vindication, leads him at last to his great theme of romantic idealism. Perhaps predictably (if we recall the unexceptionable, and unconvincing, hero of *The 'Half Moon'*), perhaps necessarily, Ford works in his masterpiece by implication and indirection. He creates a series of romantic figures, each of whom aspires to be beyond reproach. He shares in, he draws with acute and sympathetic insight, their consistently motivated personalities, and the relationship between their personalities and their various ethical values. But he never suggests in *The Good Soldier* that the ego-ideals his characters follow may be achieved, save in their own imaginations, in their self-deceptions and illusions, or should be achieved. He never asks us to believe in an incredibly good hero or to assent to an ethic that would exalt that hero at the expense either of a whole unworthy world or of all moral obligations. Ford sympathizes with his characters in *The Good Soldier*, but he has learned to judge them for their immaturity, their egoism, their foolish rejection of things as they are, and their headlong pursuit of an impossible conception of themselves.

CHAPTER 5

Parade's End

MORE OBVIOUSLY than *The Good Soldier,* the four novels *Some Do Not . . .* (1924), *No More Parades* (1925), *A Man Could Stand Up—* (1926) and *The Last Post* (1928)—all republished in the United States in 1950 as *Parade's End*—are the culmination of Ford's efforts to record and to evaluate the life of his times. In their breadth of scene and their length, these novels are reminiscent of Victorian and Edwardian social realism. They present a picture of England, particularly of upper-class England, on the brink of World War I, in the trenches of the Western Front, and in the uneasy peace that followed the Treaty of Versailles.

Parade's End covers a more ambitious range of affairs than *The Good Soldier,* and it is a frankly intellectual work. It offers numerous passages of reflection, of discussion, of argument not only about men and women—the relationship which Dowell calls "the first thing in the world" (*GS,* p. 10)—but also about English finance, politics, social reform, and the conduct of the war in Westminster and in Flanders and France. And where *The Good Soldier* works by implication, *Parade's End* is often explicit. Dowell, for example, questions the ideals and the actions of the Ashburnhams. But Valentine Wannop concludes that Edith Ethel Duchemin sincerely aspires to the virtues she can only imitate. "Valentine knew that Edith Ethel really loved beauty, circumspection, urbanity. It was no hypocrisy that made her advocate the Atalanta race of chastity."[1]

---

1. *Some Do Not . . .* in *Parade's End* (New York: Knopf, 1950),

This same shift from the implicit toward the explicit, from question toward conclusion, is evident in the whole thematic movement of the tetralogy. In the opening chapter of *Some Do Not . . .* , Christopher Tietjens, in a comically one-sided dispute with Vincent Macmaster, sets forth a scale of moral values: "I stand for monogamy and chastity. And for no talking about it. Of course if a man who's a man wants to have a woman he has her. And again, no talking about it. He'd no doubt be in the end better, and better off, if he didn't. Just as it would probably be better for him if he didn't have the second glass of whisky and soda" (*SDN*, p. 18). The ethical contrast, of course, is typically Fordian. Tietjens stands for a scrupulous fidelity to Christian morality or, as he terms it on other occasions, "saintliness" or "Anglican sainthood." But next to that ideal he prizes direct self-expression. Both of these standards of conduct he terms "clean," and he opposes them to the absolute bottom of his scale, "lachrymose polygamy," whose practitioners disguise fornication with "polysyllabic Justification by Love" and attempt to "creep" into "heaven" (*SDN*, p. 18). Such self-deceit and pretentious virtue are "filthy" and "loathsome." And Tietjens measures more than private life with his scale of values: making a success of a public career is also a "dirty business" (*SDN*, p. 17).

Tietjens' apparently incidental argument—it arises from Macmaster's casual quotation of Rossetti—prepares for all that follows. The ethical attitudes Tietjens describes are echoed and re-echoed in the course of the tetralogy and spring, again in typical Fordian fashion, from a psychological basis. Tietjens thinks, "Stoic or Epicurean; Caliph in the harem or Dervish desiccating in the sand; one or the other you must be" (*SDN*, p. 187). The tetralogy qualifies his thought to one *and* the other you must be—for the impulse toward goodness lives in the human personality side by side with the impulse toward evil. Repression of passion, more likely than not, leads to its lawless expression. The Reverend Mr. Duchemin "acquired the craving for drink when fasting, from finishing the sacramental wine after communion services" (*SDN*, p. 191). Tietjens' promiscuous wife Sylvia knows the "stimulation to be got out

---

p. 268. All subsequent references in the text will be to this edition of the novel.

of parsimonious living."[2] Valentine, after a wartime term of service in a public girls' school, "a sort of nonconformist cloister,"[3] longs for "the sea of Tibullus, of the Anthologists, of Sappho, even" (*MCSU*, p. 506). Even Tietjens, whose wish has always been for relentless self-control, has married Sylvia because he made love to her in a railway carriage.

Like these of its members, at once individual and representative, English society as Ford presents it is impelled both to goodness and evil, both to control and to express its pride, anger, jealousy, sexual passion. It subscribes officially to the Christian code of conduct. But it lives according to an intricate system of moral shifts and compromises. It pretends to virtue; it deceives itself; it goes on talking with "polite animation" (*SDN*, p. 100) as if it had never heard Mr. Duchemin's voice insistent with alcohol.

To introduce the particular compromises of his society, or rather, to expose them, is one of Ford's principal aims in *Parade's End*. Indeed, in *Some Do Not* . . . his characters so frequently take up and expand the title, the principal leitmotiv, that they virtually compose an ethical primer for gentlemen and women, witness the following quotations on love and marriage:

No gentleman thinks such things of his wife [as that she may have seduced him] (*SDN*, p. 122).

Such calamities [as a wife's infidelity] are the will of God. A gentleman accepts them (*SDN*, p. 11).

A woman who has been let down by one man has the right— has the duty for the sake of her child—to let down a man (*SDN*, p. 174).

If a man who's a gentleman suffers the begetting of his child he must, in decency, take the consequences (*SDN*, p. 176).

No one but a blackguard would ever submit a woman to the ordeal of divorce (*SDN*, p. 6).

---

2. *No More Parades* in *Parade's End*, p. 424. All subsequent references in the text will be to this edition of the novel.

3. *A Man Could Stand Up—* in *Parade's End*, p. 513. Unless otherwise noted, all subsequent references in the text will be to this edition of the novel.

There's no reason why a man shouldn't have a girl [a shopgirl, not a lady], and if he has he ought to keep her decently (*SDN*, p. 213).

The confrontation of human nature is obviously oblique, and the license allowed sexual passion arbitrary. The English "tradition," to choose one of the many words with which Ford describes society's *de facto* moral code, is a system of checks and balances; gentlemen and women may err with impunity—in certain prescribed ways.

So many rules of conduct should at least render men secure. But from the opening chapters of *Some Do Not . . .* , it is apparent that the class that "administered the world" in "nonchalant Balliol voices" (*SDN*, p. 3) is uneasy and fearful. Its order is threatened by the clamorous voices of those who share neither its responsibilities nor its privileges. In a hitherto circumspect golf club at Rye, for example, prosperous and overfed city men frankly compare the merits of Gertie and the Gitana girls, and suffragettes disturb the rituals of the game on the links. The two groups of interlopers clash with such violence that even gentlemen become involved. Tietjens hears himself threaten to knock the head off one of the city men and, "exhausted, beyond thinking or shouting" (*SDN*, p. 68), trips the policeman who reluctantly tries to arrest the girls. The final result is conflict, albeit verbal rather than physical, among gentlemen themselves:

> Mr. Sandbach refused to continue his match with Tietjens. He said that Tietjens was the sort of fellow who was the ruin of England. He said he had a good mind to issue a warrant for the arrest of Tietjens—for obstructing the course of justice. Tietjens pointed out that Sandbach wasn't a borough magistrate and so couldn't. And Sandbach went off, dot and carry one, and began a furious row with the two city men who had retreated to a distance. He said they were the sort of men who were the ruin of England (*SDN*, p. 69).

While this treatment of the disruption of tradition is primarily comic, the scene has its sinister implications.

Even when they are undisturbed by the impertinences of *nouveaux riches* and radicals, gentlemen scarcely live in amity. Their polite animation often gives way to dissent, direct contradiction, expressions of grievance, insults, or simply inattention to one another's remarks. Macmaster, Sandbach, and Tietjens are already at odds before the suffragettes and city men antagonize them. (I quote only the spoken discourse from the text):

(Macmaster to Sandbach): "Don't you know that you don't shout while a man is driving? Or haven't you played golf?"

(Sandbach to Tietjens): "Golly! That chap's got a temper!"

(Tietjens): "Only over this game. You deserved what you got."

(Sandbach): "I did. . . . But I didn't spoil his shot. He's out-driven the General twenty yards."

(Tietjens): "It would have been sixty but for you."

(Sandbach, after a pause): "By Jove, your friend is on with his second . . . You wouldn't believe it of such a *little* beggar! He's not much class, is he?"

(Tietjens): "Oh, about *our* class! He wouldn't take a bet about driving into the couple ahead."

(Sandbach): "Ah, I suppose he gets you out of scrapes with girls and the Treasury, and you take him about in return. It's a practical combination" (*SDN*, p. 64).

Often Ford's gentlemen and women reveal their hostility to one another even more directly—in such phrases as "look here," "listen here," "damn it all," and "oh no you don't."

While traditional morals and manners permit a considerable exercise of aggressive impulses, human nature is continually tempted to take still greater license. The city men—the "little competition wallah head clerks" of the government (*SDN*, p. 62) and the "beastly squits" of commerce (*SDN*, p. 161)—are, after all, merely exaggerations of the Tietjens, Macmasters, and Sandbachs, different in degree of self-expression rather than kind. As Valentine in the confines of her nonconformist cloister sums up the motivations of the ruling class, "You had to keep them—the Girls, the Populace, everybody!—in hand now, for once you let go there was no knowing where They, like waters parted from the seas, mightn't carry You" (*MCSU*, p. 511). If tradition is obviously menaced from without, it also clearly has enemies within. Order itself is always tempted to anarchy. Hence the insistence, the fervor, with which society continually voices its ethical premises and the panic with which it conceals infractions even of its own imperfect code.

Each of the novels of the tetralogy develops a major thematic movement. In *Some Do Not . . .* , Tietjens vacillates between saintliness and tradition. His wife's beauty and her recklessness, for the present, no longer tempt him. But his hopeless love for Valentine Wannop, which develops in counterpoint to Macmaster's illicit passion for Mrs. Duchemin, brings him to the edge of a clandestine affair. After the war begins, Tietjens and Valentine decide to indulge their love secretly, like Macmaster and Mrs. Duchemin, with due arrangement for the preservation of appearances, of propriety; but at the last instant they both change their minds. Tietjens, who has since left the civil service for the army, goes to France rejecting both his own initial premise of lawlessness and society's proposition of permissible vice: "If then a man who's a man wants to have a woman. . . . Damn it, he doesn't!" (*SDN*, p. 281). In his personal life, Tietjens decides for saintliness.

No More Parades, however, discovers him still a public man of tradition. In a base camp outside Rouen he trains and equips his men for the front as if he were a "Chelsea adjutant getting off a draft of the Second Coldstreams" (*NMP*, p. 399). Just as there are rules for love and marriage, so there are regulations for the proper conduct of violence. Yet when Sylvia appears in Rouen, her passion whetted by her husband's indifference, Tietjens very nearly succumbs to her attractions and hence to lawlessness. Because of his involvement with his wife, he does, in fact, strike a superior officer; and when his godfather, General Campion, puts him informally on trial and asks him why he does not rid himself of Sylvia for good, by divorce, he cannot answer. After a strained discussion in which even the General—the most stalwart defender of tradition in *Parade's End*—is "in disorder" (*NMP*, p. 474), both men take refuge from their personal difficulties in the performance, at once comic and pathetic, of army duty: they inspect Tietjens' cookhouses. Saintliness is a remote possibility. And tradition, a slim bulwark against anarchy.

In *A Man Could Stand Up—*, as psychological drama and historical event continue to interact, both Tietjens and Valentine pass beyond even the limited protection of tradition. Each of them confronts a world bereft of order and each experiences a mental strain so severe that it borders on insanity. On the morning of the Armistice, against the background of all London celebrating, Valentine controls her thoughts with difficulty and quarrels to the point of insult with Miss Wanostrocht, the prudent and prudish head of her school. Tietjens, a member now of the ragtag army at the weakest sector of the front, saves his sanity only by the memory of Valentine. They meet again, on Armistice Day, determined to live together in spite of both the old dictates of tradition and the chaos that now surrounds them. They choose to effect a new compromise between self-denial and self-expression; and *The Last Post*, carrying them into peace-time, confirms and elaborates the nature of their choice. The main thematic movement of *Parade's End*, reminiscent of *A Call* and *The Good Soldier*, is dialectical.

Ford's art is almost always equal to his ambitious purposes in *Parade's End*. Yet it should be remarked that the tetralogy is a less perfect work than *The Good Soldier*. The last two volumes, particularly, show momentary lapses in artistic control. Some flaws— for example, an awkward explanation of a time shift in Part One of *A Man Could Stand Up—(MCSU*, pp. 517-518) and a few pages of sing-song prose in *The Last Post*[4]—seem to be due simply to carelessness. Some, like a mock-heroic digression on Chantecler and Madame Partlet (*LP*, pp. 700-701), apparently proceed from an enthusiastic but inappropriate sense of whimsy. Other yieldings to old temptations, however, are more extensive and more serious. At the end of Part Two of *A Man Could Stand Up—*, Tietjens suffers two heavy strokes of sheer bad fortune. He receives a virtually unmotivated and wholly unjustifiable reproof from General Campion, and he learns that one of his junior officers was shot as he carried him to apparent safety. For the moment, Tietjens appears to be simply the innocent victim of a malevolent universe. A somewhat similar kind of simplification occurs in *The Last Post* when, at the very end, Ford sentimentalizes Sylvia. Momentary kindness, particularly kindness that springs from defiance, is typical of Sylvia. Thus when Tietjens' hired man accuses her of trying to make Valentine miscarry and she calls him a "damn fool" in

---

4. *The Last Post* in *Parade's End*, pp. 686-687. All subsequent references in the text will be to this edition of the novel.

reply and canters down the hill to announce her decision to divorce Tietjens, Sylvia is convincing. But when she says to Valentine, "I have a fine [child] but I wanted another" (*LP*, p. 827), she ceases to be the Sylvia of familiar acquaintance. Here, as in Part Two of *A Man Could Stand Up—*, Ford may be misled by excessive sympathy for his character, or he may be overstating the resolution of his forces of conflict. (Certainly *The Last Post* shows other unmistakable signs of thematic insistence, notably in the pagan and Christian symbolism with which Ford rather awkwardly overlays his narrative.) All of these moments of carelessness, of whimsy, of sentimentality, and of overstatement are, admittedly, very uncomfortable ones. But though they detract from, they certainly do not destroy an otherwise impressive performance.

For all its frank intellectuality, for all its plain social and moral concerns, *Parade's End* does not read like a Fabian tract or a paper in ethics. Just as Ford's impressionism in *The Good Soldier* achieves more than a gradual, hence lifelike, introduction to a complex set of characters, so his very similar methods in the tetralogy offer more than a record of a particular period of English life. His detached and superior narrative voice speaks intermittently throughout the series; in *Some Do Not . . .* , which primarily introduces the principal characters and their social milieu, it speaks at length. To forget the tone of this voice, to fail to note the absurd human behavior in many of the scenes it presents, and to overlook the fact that Ford's juxtapositions of episode are often funny as well as thematically significant, is to forget, as some critics have done, one of the most engaging and characteristic features of the Tietjens series. From beginning to end, *Parade's End* is, in part, social comedy. In *Some Do Not . . .* , for example, Mrs. Duchemin gives a traditionally elegant breakfast to Macmaster, Valentine, Tietjens, and a handful of other guests. In its setting of Turner paintings, old woodwork, expensive tableware, and caviar ordered from Bond Street, the scene is historically and socially accurate. But it is also broadly comic. Mrs. Duchemin's position at her own table is "strategic" (*SDN*, p. 90) and her silver chafing dishes, épergnes, and rosebowls form a "fortification" (*SDN*, p. 80)—behind which the Reverend Mr. Duchemin will presently rise to shout obscenities in his "Oxford Movement voice" (*SDN*, p. 99).

Of course, despite Ford's disposition to be explicit in *Parade's End*, he nonetheless involves us intellectually in his fiction. We need not work our way through such intricate deceits as Dowell's self-defense, but we are induced to participate, to organize the discrete, and to make complex moral judgments.

In his treatment of the recurrent themes of saintliness, self-expression, and tradition, Ford favors none of his characters with consistent sympathy or approval. As he insists in his preface to *A Man Could Stand Up—*, even Tietjens is "not, *not*, *NOT*" the author's spokesman.[5] Tietjens criticizes tradition, but he belongs to it all the same; and Ford arranges many of the incidents in *Some Do Not . . .* in order to contrast what Tietjens says with what he does. Immediately after he rudely sets his scale of values before Macmaster, Tietjens descends from the train at Ashford to confront the "extraordinarily blue, innocent eyes" of General Campion. When the General asks, "How's your mother-in-law?" Tietjens answers, "I believe she's much better. Quite restored" (*SDN*, p. 21). With these words, Tietjens supports a fiction invented to save traditional appearances. In reality, his mother-in-law has not been ill; she has gone to the Continent to disguise the fact that Sylvia has fled there with a lover. Tietjens also conceals Macmaster's affair with Mrs. Duchemin and fails to expose a fraudulently low report of French war losses that Macmaster submits to His Majesty's Ministry of Imperial Statistics.

Tietjens is neither a hypocrite nor a coward. His actions are influenced by personal loyalty—to his wife, to his friend, to his godfather. They are also influenced by a genuine attraction to the very tradition he criticizes. Like most men, in Ford's world and the real one, Tietjens is morally inconsistent. As Sylvia sums up his dilemma: "I tell you he's so formal he can't do without all the conventions there are and so truthful he can't use half of them" (*SDN*, p. 32). His inconsistency alone accounts for many of the *contretemps* he suffers.

All the principal characters of *Parade's End* may be aligned on Tietjens' moral scale. But, like Tietjens, they too are inconstant, sometimes saintly, sometimes rebellious, sometimes traditional. In-

---

5. *A Man Could Stand Up—* (New York: Albert & Charles Boni, 1926), p. vi.

deed, since Ford's attitude transcends those of his characters, the points of the scale themselves frequently change their relative positions. And, as a summary of the dialectic movement of the tetralogy has already suggested, the entire scale is finally superseded by a further definition of goodness. While the characters are in the process of living, they are also learning. Each of them at times speaks truthfully about himself, about others, about the way they all act, and about the way they should act. But their statements and their actions must always be judged by the immediate context in which they occur and by the context of the whole tetralogy.

Tietjens, Sylvia, Valentine, Mr. and Mrs. Duchemin, and Macmaster all live lives larger than their various thematic roles. They carry their ethical burdens easily, even incidentally, because they are strong in their fidelity to human nature. They compel our belief—and also our sympathy. Ford involves us emotionally as well as intellectually in the moral dilemmas of his characters; and just as in *The Good Soldier* he elicits an indulgent response to the longing for innocence, so in *Parade's End* he forces us to recognize the attractions not only of saintliness, but also of tradition and even of anarchy. The scene where Sylvia confronts Tietjens in a hotel in Rouen (Chapter II, Part Two of *No More Parades*) may serve as an extended example of the ways in which Ford utilizes his impressionist techniques to manipulate our responses to his fiction.

II

Strictly speaking, the whole tetralogy to this point has prepared for this chapter, just as the chapter in turn prepares for the rest of the tetralogy. The entire history of Sylvia's and Tietjens' marriage, as well as their changing relationship to tradition, is relevant to their wartime meeting in Rouen. One point in the previous action, however, deserves particular mention—a fragment of a conversation Sylvia has had, earlier in the day of the dramatic present, with a former lover:

[Perowne] said:
"Will you leave your bedroom door unlocked, or won't you?"
She said: [...]
"You can come. . . . I won't lock my door. But I don't say that

you'll get anything . . . or that you'll like what you get. . . . That's a fair tip. . . ." She added suddenly: "You *sale fat* . . . take what you get and be damned to you! . . ."

Major Perowne had suddenly taken to twirling his moustaches [. . .] (*NMP*, pp. 386-387).

Tietjens, in Chapter II, does not know of Sylvia's arrangements with Perowne, nor does Sylvia recall them—although her mind ranges over a number of incidents in her very near as well as her remote past. But we are forewarned of the *débâcle* that waits at the end of the evening.

Throughout the tetralogy, Ford employs three points of view. He presents dramatic action; he speaks in his narrative voice to describe character, action, and thought; and he relates thought directly, as stream of consciousness. The result is a combination of intimacy and detachment much the same as that achieved through Dowell's varying distance from his story. In Chapter II, Part Two of *No More Parades*, however, Ford restricts his narrative voice to a description of the action as Sylvia sees it and to a description of her thoughts. Hers, moreover, is the only stream of consciousness. The chapter is primarily about Sylvia, just as other parts of the tetralogy are primarily about Tietjens or Valentine or Campion or Macmaster.

The chapter opens with eight pages of continuous dramatic present as Sylvia talks, first with Tietjens' friend, Lieutenant Cowley, then with both Lieutenant Cowley and Tietjens. Her role in the conversation is, typically, disruptive. She is aware of her social superiority to Cowley, a newly commissioned officer whom she takes to be a "very trustworthy small tradesman: the grocer from round the corner whom, sometimes, you allow to supply you with paraffin" (*NMP*, p. 397); and she uses him for her own purposes. After prompting him to outline Tietjens' schedule of the day before, she answers his serious account of army routine with disbelief and scorn. Then, when he stops to defend himself, she brusquely reminds him to get on with his story. For she is pursuing "investigations" (*NMP*, p. 397). She has convinced herself that Tietjens has brought Valentine Wannop to France as his mistress; she imagines that in Cowley's "confusion," which she, of course, has induced, she may "come upon traces of Miss Wannop in Rouen" (*NMP,* p. 398). She does not; and finally, calling the lieutenant *Mr.* Cowley, she diverts the conversation to a point very close to her goal: "Of course my husband would not have time to write very full letters. . . . He is not like the giddy young subalterns who run after . . ." (*NMP,* pp. 398-399). Cowley replies with a "great roar of laughter: 'The captain run after skirts. . . . Why, I can number on my hands the times he's been out of my sight since he's had the battalion! ' " (*NMP,* p. 399).

When Tietjens appears, Sylvia continues her disruptive course. Tietjens announces that he must return to camp before 4.30 a.m.; Sylvia cuts him off with: "Isn't there a poem . . . '*Ah me, the dawn, the dawn, it comes too soon!*' . . . said of course by lovers in bed? . . . Who was the poet?" (*NMP,* p. 400). Tietjens explains to Cowley that he has not been able to find an officer to march his draft. He then answers Sylvia with a brief lecture on the medieval aubade. The pattern continues. Cowley and Tietjens, although Tietjens speaks less often, discourse along serious and sequential lines, while Sylvia repeatedly turns everything to her personal aims. With a number of *doubles entendres,* which Cowley does not understand, she taunts Tietjens with his continence toward her, his love for Valentine, his protection of the Macmasters—with, in short, almost every subject that troubles his conscience. Then, mocking him with his aspirations to saintliness, she says to Cowley: "He helped virtuous Scotch students, and broken down gentry. . . . And women taken in adultery. . . . All of them. . . . Like . . . You know Who. . . . That is his model. . . ." (*NMP,* p. 404).

Her conversational role, predictable only in its unpredictability, is repeated in the riot of Sylvia's thoughts. When she completes her investigations, when she is sure that Tietjens is so occupied with the army that he could not possibly keep Valentine in Rouen, she is not pleased but depressed. The narrative voice explains her unexpected reaction: "The morality of these matters is this: If you have an incomparably beautiful woman on your hands you must occupy yourself solely with her. . . . Nature exacts that of you . . . until you are unfaithful to her with a snubnosed girl with freckles; that, of course, being a reaction, is still in a way occupying yourself with your woman! . . . But to betray her with a battalion . . . That is against decency, against Nature. . . ." (*NMP,* p. 399). The logical exposition, the reference to "morality," the derivation of rule from Nature, emphasizes by ironic contrast Sylvia's unreasonable preoccupations and evaluations of experience. Her idiosyncrasy is evident again in her reaction to Tietjens' disquisition on the aubade. She thinks Tietjens has assumed his "slow pomposity" (*NMP*, p. 400) in order to cover Cowley's embarrassment at her reference to lovers in bed; she "hate[s]" her husband's thoughtfulness. Yet, the next moment, "emotion was going all over Sylvia . . . at the proximity of Tietjens" (*NMP*, p. 400). Her explanation of Tietjens' motive is incomplete. He *has* protected Cowley, but he has also ignored her obvious invitation to love. His apparent indifference has aroused her passion—and her passion leads her, perversely, to torment him further.

Sylvia's stream of consciousness reveals still further unreason. She "*can't* help" making her remarks (*NMP*, p. 401). She calls on the heavenly powers to protect her as well as Tietjens from her passion and tries, in vain, to read the significance of her own actions, as if they were omens. She begs for a sign that her husband will come back to her. When her own memory supplies unbidden a sign to the contrary, she thinks: "Blessed Mary! You've given it me in the neck. . . . Yet you could not name a father for your child, and I can name two. . . . I'm going mad. . . . Both I and he are going to go mad. . . ." (*NMP*, p. 404).

After this momentary climax, Ford stops the clock of his present action, moves it forward, and starts it again: "[Sylvia] made in the smoking-room, whilst she was waiting for both Tietjens and Cowley to come back from the telephone, another pact, this time with Father Consett in heaven!" (*NMP*, p. 405). Then, after just a few lines in which Sylvia thinks about Father Consett, who had once been her spiritual adviser, Ford begins a series of time shifts to past action. The convention he successfully adopts here, as elsewhere in the tetralogy, is that his character, in this case Sylvia, is remembering the past. (Her memory, of course, supplies a full transcript of certain scenes, just as Dowell's narration does in *The Good Soldier*. Fortunately for the scope of his art, Ford does not adhere rigidly to his theoretical canon of verisimilitude but employs, in his shifts to the past, the same combination of drama, narrative voice, and stream of consciousness that he uses in the dramatic present.) The direction of her memory is apparently random, apparently associational. In fact, however, the sequence is one of cause and effect; the whole series of time-shifts reveals the reasons why Sylvia makes her pact with Father Consett. Indeed, the narrative voice, without violating the convention that Sylvia is remembering, from time to time calls attention to the causal sequence by its use of the words of logical argument. The series of time shifts begins (the italics are mine):

> She was by that time [the time when she makes the pact] fairly calm again. You cannot keep up fits of emotion by the hour. At any rate, with her, the fits of emotion were periodical and unexpected, though her colder passion remained always the same. . . . *Thus,* when Christopher had come into Lady Sachse's that afternoon, she had been perfectly calm (*NMP,* p. 405).

The afternoon at Lady Sachse's both repeats and intensifies the patterns of action and reaction which Sylvia has already exhibited in conversation with Cowley and Tietjens. The account of the afternoon has scarcely begun when two brief shifts to a slightly earlier past show the disruptive nature of her behavior even when she is perfectly calm. She has been standing at the party with her former lover, Perowne, and has thereby distressed General Campion. She has also helped to frustrate the General's hope that the party "might do something to cement the Entente Cordiale" (*NMP,* p. 405) by giving a French marquis a "long cold glance" that "extinguished" him (*NMP,* p. 406). At the same time, as a third shift backward reveals, she has been pursuing a characteristic occupation: she has appraised all the men in the gathering and noted that not a single one is "presentable" (*NMP,* p. 406).

With Tietjens' arrival, her peace of mind vanishes and she wars against convention with increasing vigor. When Tietjens assures General Campion that he has already seen his wife since her arrival in Rouen—a lie by implication—Sylvia experiences a "first wave of emotion" (*NMP,* p. 406). When Tietjens, who has just saved his personal situation, goes on to save the social situation by placating a disagreeable French duchess, Sylvia has had as much as she can "bear" (*NMP,* p. 409). She decides to tell the General that Tietjens is a Socialist. As two brief forward shifts in time relate, she regrets her decision as soon as she has carried it out and continues to regret it much later. Nonetheless, at the party she adds a second indictment of Tietjens to her first. "'He desires,' Sylvia said, and she had no idea when she said it, 'to model himself upon our Lord. . . .'" (*NMP*, p. 412).

Ford returns from the afternoon to the evening with a further emphasis on Sylvia's motives. The narrative voice begins (the italics are mine), "*So*, sitting there, in the smoking-lounge of the hotel [. . .]" (*NMP*, p. 412); interjects a brief but breathless summary of Sylvia's reactions to her surroundings, to Lieutenant Cowley, to Macmaster; then finishes its original sequence: "*So*, sitting there, she made a new pact, this time with Father Consett in heaven" (*NMP*, p. 413). The narrative voice explains why Sylvia calls on Father Consett rather than any other of her heavenly powers: "Father Consett was very much in her mind, *for* she was very much in the midst of the British military authorities who had hanged him" (*NMP*, p. 413). And Sylvia's stream of consciousness supplies the terms of her pact: if in ten minutes she finds a presentable man in the room, she will leave Tietjens and go into a convent for the rest of her life.

The over-all pattern of her motives has been a balance of grievances against concessions, of injuries inflicted against restitutions proposed. Even her brief thoughts on Cowley and Macmaster flow in a pattern of pro and con. "For long years she had put up with Tietjens' protégé, the odious Sir Vincent Macmaster, at all sorts of meals and all sorts of places . . . but of course that was only Christopher's rights . . . to have in his own house, which, in the circumstances, wasn't morally hers, any snuffling, nervous, walrus-moustached or orientally obsequious protégé that he chose to patronize" (*NMP*, p. 413). Sylvia is herself vaguely aware of the way in which her mind moves. She is also vaguely guilty about her treatment of Tietjens. And she suspects that the atonement she plans to make *if* the priest fulfills the terms of her pact is inadequate. "But the real point is, father," she asks, "Is it sporting? . . . Sporting or whatever it is?" (*NMP*, p. 416).

The nature and arrangement of Ford's events, the periodic detachment of his narrative voice and its ruthless logical stress on the unreasonable, even irrational, sequence of Sylvia's "game"—all invite an unfavorable judgment of his heroine. Sylvia will accept no discipline from society; and the discipline she imposes on herself—the cultivation of her beauty, the exercise of her body, her close scrutiny of men and women—she uses only to disrupt whatever order she perceives in the world around her—army routine, social protocol, even so simple an activity of intellect as the pursuit of an intelligible conversation. She is a passionate woman, but her passion is roused only by resistance. Hence her lack of interest in the men who importune her and her obsession with Tietjens, who is apparently indifferent: his self-control is an insistent provocation to her impulse toward anarchic self-expression. Although she does seem to possess a rudimentary sense of justice, her occasional kindnesses invariably arise from ambivalent motives—her pact with Father Consett is made as much in defiance of British authority as it is in atonement to Tietjens. Her whole nature, in short, is bent on destruction. As Tietjens had observed in *Some Do Not* . . . , "If you wanted something killed you'd go to Sylvia Tietjens in the sure faith that she would kill it: emotion, hope, ideal; kill it quick and sure" (*SDN*, p. 128). And her impulse to kill she ultimately directs against herself. To seduce Tietjens in Rouen is her most ardent wish but one: to fail to seduce him.

Yet this cruel, illogical, highly neurotic woman is extremely *sympathique*. Ford leads us to recognize and remember Sylvia's faults, but he also forces us to share them. Or, more precisely, to share some of them and forgive the rest. By the end of the chapter, indeed, we have been drawn so far into complicity with Sylvia that we virtually become for a time advocates of anarchy.

Even in Part One of *No More Parades*, where he elicits a sympathetic response to Tietjens' efforts to bring order out of the military confusion and incompetence around him, Ford reveals the double nature of army life. Much of it is heroic, but much is simply petty:

> The drafts moved off, unknotting themselves like snakes, coiling out of inextricable bunches, sliding vertebrately over the mud to dip into their bowls—the rabbis found Jews dying to whom to administer; the vets, spavined mules; the V.A.D.s, men without jaws and shoulders in C.C.C.s; the camp-cookers, frozen beef; the chiropodists, ingrowing toenails; the dentists,

decayed molars; the naval howitzers, camouflaged emplace-
ments in picturesquely wooded dingles. . . . (*NMP*, p. 331).

And it is the pettiness and self-importance of army discipline
that he chooses to stress in Chapter II, Part Two. So Sylvia's contemptuous responses to Cowley's comically ponderous and slow-
witted iteration of routine seem quite appropriate. Tietjens and
Cowley, with their humorless concern for the army's feet and the
army's toothbrushes, *do* seem to resemble, as Sylvia thinks, "school-
boys" performing the rituals of a pointless game (*NMP*, p. 398).
When Sylvia cuts off Cowley's parrot-like report of one of Tietjens'
maxims: "He says that no draft he turns out shall. . . ." (*NMP*,
p. 398), her interruption is agreeably rude. Tietjens *is*, at times,
pedantic. In the conversation that follows he *does* play, as Sylvia
thinks to herself, the "pompous ass" (*NMP*, p. 400).

In his shift back to the afternoon at Lady Sachse's, Ford presents and mocks another kind of game. A young French noble-
man is a "shade too theatrical" (*NMP*, p. 405). General Campion
is "running the show pretty strong" (*NMP*, p. 405) for the sake
of Anglo-French relations. Tietjens "staged his meeting" with Sylvia (*NMP*, p. 406). Indeed, the whole scene reveals an absurd
respect for appearances, for social ceremony. The affair is a traditional display, and with it Ford extends the scope of tradition beyond a strictly English society:

> The undissolvable air of the eighteenth century that the
> French contrive to retain in all their effects kept the scene
> singularly together. On a sofa sat the duchess, relatives leaning
> over her. She was a duchess with one of those impossible
> names: Beauchain-Radigutz or something like it. The bluish
> room was octagonal and vaulted, up to a rosette in the centre
> of the ceiling. English officers and V.A.D.s of some evident
> presence opened out to the left, French military and very
> black-clothed women of all ages, but all apparently widows,
> opened out to the right, as if the duchess shone down a sea at
> sunset. Beside her on the sofa you did not see Lady Sachse;
> leaning over her you did not see the prospective bride. This
> stoutish, unpresentable, coldly venomous woman, in black
> clothes so shabby that they might have been grey tweed, ex-
> tinguished other personalities as the sun conceals planets. A

fattish, brilliantined personality, in mufti, with a scarlet rosette, stood sideways to the duchess's right, his hands extended forward as if in an invitation to the dance. (*NMP*, p. 407)

The scene is viewed through Sylvia's eyes and we share her amusement. We also sympathize with her destructive behavior because, while she strikes at Tietjens—a personal impulse—she also pricks the balloon of pride and pretension—a universal impulse. And the tradition she flouts is, after all, a social order that is morally corrupt. The afternoon at Lady Sachse's is comic throughout, but, like the scene on the golf course at Rye, it has serious overtones.

When Tietjens assures General Campion that he has already seen Sylvia, he deliberately speaks and acts to create the impression that he and his wife are on good terms. The disagreeable duchess delays the ceremony, whose primary object in any event is a hard marriage bargain, in order to drive a still harder bargain in coal. She and Tietjens together make an agreement "at the pit-head prices of the Middlesbrough-Cleveland district as the prices were on the 3rd of August, nineteen fourteen" (*NMP*, p. 409). They act, in other words, as if the war had never taken place. Pretense, greed, evasion of fact—their manifestations here may be minor. But tradition is designed to permit and to shield their more egregious and more harmful exercise. Tietjens' "lie" recalls other deceits he has practiced. The elegance of Lady Sachse's appointments recalls various scenes from *Some Do Not . . .* , the Duchemin breakfast for one. The geometric disposition of the guests, in particular, brings to mind an afternoon in Gray's Inn when Edith Ethel Duchemin, since become Lady Macmaster, administered a deliberate snub to Valentine's aging mother, whereas Sylvia greeted Mrs. Wannop with exceptional courtesy.

Ford brings his series of time shifts to conclusion with a superbly broad, climactic reminder of the distance that separates the morality of tradition from unequivocal goodness:

"He desires," Sylvia said, and she had no idea when she said it, "to model himself upon our Lord. . . ."

The general leant back in the sofa. He said almost indulgently: "Who's that . . . our *Lord*?"

Sylvia said:

"Upon our Lord Jesus Christ. . . ."

He sprang to his feet as if she had stabbed him with a hatpin.
"Our . . ." he exclaimed. "Good God! . . . I always knew he
had a screw loose. . . . But . . ." He said briskly: "Give all his
goods to the poor! . . . But He wasn't a . . . Not a Socialist! What
was it He said: Render unto Caesar . . . It wouldn't be necessary
to drum Him out of the army . . ." He said: "Good Lord! . . .
Good Lord! . . . Of course his poor dear mother was a little . . .
But, hang it! . . . The Wannop girl! . . ." Extreme discomfort
overcame him. . . . (*NMP*, p. 412)

Within the controlling framework of his motivational sequence,
then, Ford places scenes that emphasize the vanity, the selfishness,
and the sham of established order. The marriage of the psychological and the ethical interests is a fruitful one, for Sylvia and
tradition work to reveal each other.

Sylvia's appropriate reactions to tradition, however, are only
one means by which Ford evokes an indulgent response to his
heroine. Another incentive to sympathy is, quite simply, point of
view. The narrative voice varies in the degree of its detachment.
There are moments when, ceasing to stand away from Sylvia, it
looks at society with her. When such a diminution of distance
occurs, as it does in the description of the French duchess and
her relatives, we are drawn into identification with Sylvia. Stream
of consciousness, of course, works to the same end. Intimacy alone
may not evoke sympathy, but in conjunction with other appeals
it becomes a powerful inducement to it.[6]

Having cultivated, then, a response to his heroine that is affectionate as well as critical, Ford employs Sylvia to illuminate a
further and far more sinister aspect of tradition. General Campion's
discomfiture at Lady Sachse's salon forms the climax to the first
part of Chapter II, Part Two of *No More Parades*. The remainder

---

6. I am mindful here of Leon Edel's experience with *Pilgrimage*.
Edel says (in his *Psychological Novel 1900-1950* [New York & Philadelphia: Lippincott, 1955]) that, despite Dorothy Richardson's use of stream
of consciousness, he was unable to identify with Miriam, even to find
her interesting, until he finally "saw" her through the masculine reactions
of the German pastor. The conclusion Edel draws—that stream of
consciousness does not in itself result in identification—is, I think, a sound
one.

of the chapter builds to a second and final climax. And Sylvia's relationship to the world around her undergoes various significant changes. Initially, Ford places his heroine in clear opposition to society; she is scornful and unruly, the outraged and outrageous guest of ceremony. With his first prolonged return to the dramatic present, however, he begins to reveal not the differences between Sylvia and tradition but their essential community.

As Sylvia makes her defiant pact with Father Consett, she returns to her initial metaphor for Tietjens and his fellows and qualifies it. She still sees His Majesty's officers and men as school-boys, but she can no longer dismiss them as merely self-important. Seen in clear detail, they are "sinister, hobbledehoy, waiting in the corners of playgrounds to torture someone, weak and unfortu-nate . . . . In one or other corner of their world-wide playground they had come upon Father Consett and hanged him" (*NMP*, p. 414). And Sylvia's mind repeatedly juxtaposes her own conduct with that of a society organized for war. No doubt, she thinks, Father Consett has forgiven his hangmen. "That is what you would say, father . . . Have mercy on them, for they know not what they do. . . ." She continues, "Then have mercy on me, for half the time I don't know what I'm doing!" (*NMP*, p. 415) She tries, then, to blame her actions, and incidentally those of the Kaiser's officers and men, on external forces. Perhaps Father Consett put a spell on her once when she met him at Lobscheid. Perhaps Lobscheid itself, according to Father Consett the last stronghold of paganism, infected her, and Germany, with its ancient wickedness. A few moments later, her stream of consciousness, moving closer to the margin of unconscious thought, shifts once to her immediate past, once again to her much earlier past:

> "When I saw Christopher . . . Last night? . . . Yes, it *was* last night. . . . Turning back to go up that hill. . . . And I had been talking about him to a lot of grinning private soldiers. . . . To *madden* him. . . . You *mustn't* make scenes before the ser-vants. . . . A heavy man, tired . . . come down the hill and lumbering up again. . . . There was a searchlight turned on him just as he turned. . . . I remembered the white bulldog I thrashed on the night before it died. . . . A tired, silent beast . . . With a fat white behind. . . . Tired out . . . You couldn't see its tail

because it was turned down, the stump. . . . A great, silent
beast. . . . The vet said it had been poisoned with red lead by
burglars. . . . It's beastly to die of red lead. . . . It eats up the
liver. . . . And you think you're getting better for a fortnight.
And you're always cold . . . freezing in the blood-vessels. . . .
And the poor beast had left its kennel to try and be let into
the fire. . . . And I found it at the door when I came in from
a dance without Christopher. . . . And got the rhinoceros whip
and lashed into it. There's a pleasure in lashing into a naked
white beast. . . ." (*NMP*, pp. 416-417).

This is Ford's plainest exposure of Sylvia's sadism. But its place in
the narrative suggests that her behavior, idiosyncratic and neurotic
as it is, is uncomfortably close to that of organized society. The
parallel between the "sinister schoolboys" and Sylvia is obvious.[7]

In the remainder of the chapter, Ford proceeds, as it were, to
rewrite in greater detail and with increasing intensity, his heroine's
complex relationship to society. A letter from Christopher's brother,
Mark, which Tietjens reads and Sylvia remembers, along with a
second series of recollections of time past, once again establishes
Sylvia in opposition to tradition. The distance and logical language
of the narrative voice compel us to remember the cruel pattern of
her motives, while the nature of the narrative itself continues to
draw forth a sympathetic response. Back in London, Sylvia had
learned that Tietjens was hospitalized in Rouen. The news had
aggravated her desire to hurt her husband; so she went to see
Mark and told him Valentine had had a child by Tietjens. Sylvia's ill
will and her readiness to bear false witness are, to be sure, disagreeable. But in his letter to Tietjens, Mark abuses Sylvia with the
epithets "your —— of a wife," "that baggage," "that rouged piece,"
"the party," "the trollop," "that monstrosity you honour with your
name," and "the discreditable daughter" (*NMP*, pp. 418-419). We
react, at the very least, against Mark's simplification of a complex
personality. Very probably, we also react against his vulgarity and
his eager contempt. Sylvia is the enemy of tradition, but she is

---

7. Ambrose Gordon, Jr., remarks on Sylvia's "curious affinity" with
war and notes that Ford "develop[s] her line of destruction in counterpoint with that of war" ("A Diamond of Pattern: The War of F. Madox
Ford," *Sewanee Review*, LXX [Summer, 1962], 476).

also its victim. Indeed, her position as an outcast is strengthened by the scenes she now recollects. They show her sleepless and alone, walking in St. James's Park, passing Mark's windows at dawn, watching the Wannop house, hoping to get a glimpse of the woman her husband loves.

As the narrative returns to the smoking room in Rouen, Sylvia's loneliness is, for the moment, accentuated by a multiplicity of dramatic events. The heavenly powers, as she thinks, betray her. They even seem to mock her attempt to make amends to Tietjens. There is no presentable man in the room; there is scarcely a man in the room, since an air raid has emptied it. Sylvia tries to read this "omen." Must she also, she wonders, "war" against heaven? (*NMP*, p. 426). But she cannot pursue a connected train of thought.

The noise of the air raid that has already begun increases. An orderly interrupts Tietjens with a handful of battalion reports. He also requests emergency leave to marry before his child is born. A telephone call warns that a mysterious horseman has been seen near the site of a neighboring artillery dump. The orderly announces that McKechnie, Tietjens' second-in-command, has had another nervous breakdown. The disagreeable duchess writes that the French government forbids the import of coal for greenhouses. Tietjens' draft, which has repeatedly been ordered ready and countermanded, is once again detailed to leave at dawn. Cowley, who has drunk too much brandy, enters on a long rehearsal of battle experiences. He tells Sylvia how he saw Tietjens fall in a moonlit attack; he reminds Tietjens of O Nine Morgan, who was killed after Tietjens refused him leave; he tells of his own temptations to wound himself so that he might be invalided home. A gramophone starts to play, a voice to sing cheap love songs.

Sylvia is overwhelmed by successive waves of frustration, jealousy, and rage—because she cannot torment Tietjens without interruption, because she cannot share his fellowship with officers and other ranks, because she cannot even understand his affection for men of inferior social status. These are feelings we neither share nor sanction. But Sylvia has other responses that command agreement and approval. She perceives Tietjens' private agony. She imagines the "infinitely spreading welter of pain, going away to an eternal horizon of night" (*NMP*, p. 438). And she alone comes close to a

vision of the irrationality of war. "In heaven's name," she asks
herself, "what hypocrisy, or what inconceivable chicken-heartedness
was this? They promoted this beanfeast of carnage for their own
ends; they caused the deaths of men in inconceivable holocausts
of pain and terror. Then they had crises of agony over the death
of one single man" (*NMP*, p. 438). A moment later, she sees herself
no longer an outcast, but a part of the world around her:

> The tumult increased to an incredible volume: even the thrillings
> of the near-by gramophone of two hundred horse-power, or
> whatever it was, became mere shimmerings of a gold thread
> in a drab fabric of sound. She screamed blasphemies that she
> was hardly aware of knowing. She had to scream against the
> noise; she was no more responsible for the blasphemy than if
> she had lost her identity under an anæsthetic. She *had* lost her
> identity. . . . She was one of this crowd! (*NMP*, pp. 439-440)

Ford has prepared for this climax not only throughout the chapter but from the beginning of his tetralogy. Society's system of
checks and balances, its regulation of what a gentleman does and
does not do, is at best a ruthless order, and a vulnerable one. As
Ford's language and all his events have emphasized, Sylvia's pattern
of action has always been similar to that of the class that administers
the world. Sylvia belongs to that class by nature as well as birth,
and the game she plays is an intensification of society's game. When
Sylvia works out the "rights" and "wrongs" of her private campaign
of torment:

> If, after she had been off with another man, she asked this one
> still to extend to her the honour of his name and the shelter of
> his roof, she had no right to object to his terms. Her only decent
> revenge on him was to live afterwards with such equanimity
> as to let him know the mortification of failure (*SDN*, p. 154)

—when she works out these rules, she reasons very like Mark
Tietjens outlining the "decent" way to conduct an illicit affair or
Christopher Tietjens explaining the "correct" means of dispensing
governmental patronage. Even Sylvia's habitual conversation is
in part only an exaggeration of certain gentlemanly exchanges.
Her scorn, her rudeness, and her penchant for contradiction and
interruption are reminiscent of Tietjens and Sandbach conversing

on the golf course. In a sense, Ford's society has always been organized for war. The historical events of 1914-18 and after were always implicit in tradition.

The conduct of literal war is, furthermore, only the penultimate "achievement" of tradition. Its ultimate "goal" is its own destruction. With his habitual seriousness and pedantry, Tietjens explains to Sylvia that he and his colleagues in Rouen "keep the thing going" (*NMP*, p. 431). But Sylvia, who sees for the moment more clearly, knows that the tumult of falling bombs, conflicting directives, hotel amours, madness, drunkenness, and temptations to treason signals the total breakdown of order and the end of control. She sees, quite rightly, her own anarchy mirrored in the world around her.

In his article on the tetralogy, Robie Macauley draws a significant distinction between Ford's work and that of other novelists who emerged from World War I. For the realists Barbusse, Zweig, Remarque, Hemingway, Aldington, Sassoon, "war is a terrible thing . . . it destroys minds, bodies and character." But for Ford, war is "an effect or a symptom, not a cause."[8] In the light of *A Man Could Stand Up—* and *The Last Post*, the statement might well be amended to read "an effect or a symptom *and* a cause." But Macauley's distinction remains close to the mark, and it is immensely to Ford's credit, both as an historical observer and as a psychologist.

Through Sylvia, then, Ford exposes the destructive tendencies inherent in tradition. At the same time, he draws us into a temporary commitment to anarchy. After she realizes her community with the crowd, Sylvia pours herself a glass of brandy and drinks it off "with a special intention" (*NMP*, p. 442). She abandons herself completely, in other words, to the expression of her own desires. And her recklessness seems excusable, perhaps even justifiable. In the nightmare world of Rouen, Sylvia's conviction that she cannot help what she does finally becomes her most powerful claim to sympathy. The temptation to disown responsibility, to disown it, particularly, in a time of social chaos, is surely universal enough to evoke an indulgent response. For the moment, we too become members of that crowd.

---

8. "The Good Ford," *Kenyon Review*, XI (Spring, 1949), 281. Portions of this essay appear in Macauley's "Introduction" to *Parade's End*.

But only for the moment. In the following chapter, which covers events of the next morning, Ford reveals, at intervals and almost incidentally, that Perowne has come, that Tietjens has fought with him and insulted a general, that Tietjens must in consequence be transferred from the base camp to the front. Tietjens remembers Sylvia the night before and thinks, "One is going to that fine and secret place. . . . Why not have?" (*NMP*, p. 476) But he knows, once and for all, that Sylvia offers not fulfillment but torment, and he tells General Campion that, although he will not divorce his wife, he has decided to separate from her. We consent to this rejection of Sylvia, but only with difficulty. Because we have sympathized with Sylvia, the judgment against self-expression is perforce personal and reluctant. So, in other parts of *Parade's End*, are the judgments against saintliness and against tradition.

III

As Sylvia's adventures in Rouen suggest, Ford's familiar "story" appears in *Parade's End*. Sylvia in her cruelty resembles Leonora and Nancy. Perhaps even more strikingly, she represents a fuller development of the lady of faerie, of Anne Jeal, and of the inhuman side of the heroine in *The Inheritors*. Leonora and Nancy are, or at least might have been, capable of love. But Sylvia is capable only of passion, and her passion is incidental to her game of destruction. Any relationship she enters is doomed by her very nature. She cannot be changed; she can only be avoided. In effect, Ford has split his independent heroine—into Sylvia, who kills, and Valentine, who cures. The literal inhumanity of the heroines of *The Young Lovell, The 'Half Moon'*, and *The Inheritors* now finds a human and psychologically convincing counterpart in Sylvia's sado-masochism. And it is Valentine who undergoes the bitterness of Leonora and the disillusion and guilt of Nancy—undergoes them less severely and fulfills her potential capacity for love.

Tietjens, too, reflects familiar Fordian patterns of character. He is "indicted" by society for "crimes" he doesn't commit; he is discredited in the civil service and the army; he undergoes strenuous mental and physical ordeals at the front. In these aspects of his career, he brings to mind other of Ford's brave protagonists. Like Katharine Howard, and the Young Lovell, Tietjens also is an egoist who aspires, at times, to impossible goodness. And in his relationship to Sylvia, Tietjens is reminiscent of Edward Ashburnham. He has on occasion expressed his passion for Sylvia, and he finally restrains it only with difficulty.[9]

Many of Ford's earlier conceptions of personality appear, then, in his tetralogy. At the same time, though, there are major differences between his treatment of psychology in *The Good Soldier* and in *Parade's End*. More forthright in its themes than *The Good Soldier*, *Parade's End* is also more explicit in its characterization. The narrative voice is ready to summarize and to interpret behavior and motive. And Tietjens, Sylvia, and Valentine, since they do achieve moments of self-knowledge, sometimes interpret themselves. They are more aware of what they are and what they do than Edward, Leonora, Nancy, and Dowell; and Tietjens and Valentine at least are finally more resilient. Intimate psychological exploration, moreover, figures less prominently in *Parade's End* than it does in *The Good Soldier*. The final crisis of Tietjens' attraction to Sylvia, for example, occurs off-stage, after the meeting in Rouen, and Tietjens recalls it only very briefly. And Valentine's introduction to the realities of love, through Edith Ethel Duchemin's affair with Macmaster, occupies far fewer pages than Nancy's disillusionment with "good people." Ford had a large canvas to fill in *Parade's End* and he seems, naturally enough, to have chosen to work more quickly and in bolder outline than he did in *The Good Soldier*.

Two further changes in the psychology of *Parade's End* may arise specifically from Ford's moral aims. *The Good Soldier* is a story of passion. It is also a story of Dowell's inadequate efforts to reason through moral problems.[10] The second aspect of the earlier

---

9. In certain respects, Tietjens resembles Ford's diffident heroes. He leaves Valentine, for example, at the door of her home. But the resemblance is a superficial one, a matter of what happens rather than why. Despite Sylvia's accusations, Tietjens does not lack masculinity. The accusations, as well as the sexual imagery in the sadistic whipping scene, tell us a great deal about Sylvia, but not, I think, about Tietjens. *Parade's End* does not have a diffident hero.

10. Samuel Hynes discusses this aspect of Dowell's narrative in "The Epistemology of *The Good Soldier*," *Sewanee Review*, LXIX (Spring, 1961), 225-235. Hynes is convincing, I think, except when he argues that Dowell's "fallibility" is the "norm" of the novel (p. 228).

novel reappears in *Parade's End* with a good deal of elaboration and far more emphasis. In *Some Do Not . . .* , at a moment when Sylvia thinks she will never see Tietjens again, she dares to confront him with a summary evaluation of his moral character: "Be proud when you die because of your honour. But, God, you be humble about . . . your errors in judgment" (*SDN*, p. 173). Like most other opinions voiced in *Parade's End*, this one tells a partial truth and requires amplification. Nonetheless, Sylvia's choice of words is significant. *Parade's End* is in part a story of errors in *judgment*. And as he develops this more classical psychological interest, Ford places two of his major characters less at the mercy of irrational drives than their counterparts in *The Good Soldier*. Valentine and Tietjens share in diminished degree Sylvia's impulse toward anarchy, Mr. Duchemin's asceticism, McKechnie's paranoia. But what they do is usually influenced by what they think as well as what they feel. Their behavior is in part intellectually determined and, as Sylvia's opinion suggests, that determination is not always for the best. In the rest of this chapter, I propose to turn to Ford's view of reason in *Parade's End* and to the relationship between that view and his own technique.

Compared to most other novels in the realistic tradition, the pace of *Parade's End* is fast. It does not offer, like *The Forsyte Saga*, an unhurried progression from generation to generation. Nor is it, though it may from one angle be viewed as the education of Christopher Tietjens, a leisurely *Bildungsroman*. The time of its dramatic present is short. Its years pass in a moment, between chapters or between parts; their main events are recalled now, in the present. Ford chooses to develop brief periods of time and to fill his time with events, for one of his main intents is to reveal the sheer strain of experience. His characters carry simultaneously the burden of past, present, and future—or, more accurately, they labor under this burden. Despite his use of stream of consciousness, Ford rarely records the atoms as they fall. In *Parade's End*, the mind is habitually active. Its memories are insistent; the data of its senses, peremptory. The mind, Ford would say, by its very nature grapples with experience. It engages in a ceaseless effort to order and evaluate the world which it perceives and remembers.

Sheer intellection is a pleasure. "It was in that way [Tietjens'] mind worked when he was fit: it picked up little pieces of definite, workmanlike information. When it had enough it classified them: not for any purpose, but because to know things was agreeable and gave a feeling of strength, of having in reserve something that the other fellow would not suspect. . . ." (*SDN*, p. 70). The frustration of intellection or its failure is, conversely, acutely painful. Sylvia's illogic, which she sometimes employs deliberately, is one of her most effective instruments of torture. She talks "cleverly, with imbecility; with maddening inaccuracy" (*SDN*, p. 121).

It is not surprising, then, that saintliness, in the various forms in which Tietjens imagines it, always meets two conditions. It satisfies the human aspiration to goodness and it simultaneously fulfills the human need for intellectual order. In a half-humorous, half-serious picture of heaven, Tietjens fancies God as "a great English Land-owner, benevolently awful, a colossal duke who never left his study and was thus invisible, but knowing all about the estate down to the last hind at the home farm and the last oak." And he fancies Christ as "an almost too benevolent Land-Steward, son of the Owner, knowing all about the estate down to the last child at the porter's lodge" (*NMP*, pp. 365-366). The saintly world is tightly organized, closely directed by omniscience. It therefore yields its nature to the lesser mind of man; it can be understood.

Like the imaginary world of saintliness, the real world of tradition also seeks to solace man's hunger for intellectual order. The Balliol voices utter prescriptions for every conceivable phase of life. Just as there are right and wrong ways to take a mistress, conduct a career, and curry the favor of the press, so there are proper and improper ways to choose one's friends, address one's servants, lay one's table, and ornament one's drawing-room. One of the chief aims of so much regimentation is the creation of a world with a high degree of predictability. As a boy in Port Leith, Mac-master is able to plan the steps of his career—Clifton, Cambridge, the civil service—with the certainty that he will eventually achieve "distinction, security and the quiet admiration of those around him" (*SDN*, p. 13). Tietjens, with his greater intelligence and his larger knowledge of society, can plot much more intricate sequences of human action and reaction. He foretells, with absolute accuracy, all that follows his and Sylvia's removal to Gray's Inn—down to the precise detail that Sylvia's wealthy cousin Rugely will, as he does, favor Sylvia with the highest mark of his social regard, the loan of the Rugely box at the opera.

As Tietjens says, "Principles [and the meaning of the word may be extended to include principles of manners as well as morals] are like a skeleton map of a country—you know whether you're going east or north" (*SDN*, p. 144). In addition to its other passions, society has a passion for intellectual certainty. And to this passion alone it allows free rein. "Did you think Dreyfus was guilty?" Tietjens asks General Campion. "Hang it," the General replies, "he was worse than guilty—the sort of fellow you couldn't believe in and yet couldn't prove anything against. The curse of the world. . . ." (*SDN*, p. 75). In traditional society, the ultimate enemy is the man who frustrates inquiry and defies evaluation.

In the temporal world, as opposed to the saintly world, the human demand for certainty entails multiple compromises. Just as tradition pretends to virtue that it does not possess, so it lays claim to knowledge that it does not and cannot have. But this is to anticipate Ford's conclusions. He is ready to document his case against intellectual pride, and the numerous articles of his proof are worth examination. From *Some Do Not . . .* to *The Last Post*, Ford repeatedly creates various definable patterns of thought. These patterns differ in length as in kind: sometimes they continue for only a sentence or two, sometimes for a paragraph or group of paragraphs. Yet they are all alike in one respect. They show the mind at work upon experience and, taken together, they achieve no less than a common sense critique of reason.

With certain of his patterns of thought—I shall consider them the first of two main groups—Ford chooses to lay his emphasis somewhat more on experience than on the mind, on the perceived rather than the perceiver. He places his individuals face to face with an external world that is immense and immensely complicated. Merely to attempt to grasp its size and its details is a formidable task for the mind. Thus Tietjens' view of a draft he prepares to send to the front:

> The advanced wave of the brown tide of men was already at his feet. The extraordinary complications of even the simplest

lives . . . A fellow was beside him . . . Private Logan, formerly, of all queer things for a Canadian private, a trooper of the Inniskillings; owner, of all queer things, of a milk-walk or a dairy farm, outside Sydney, which is in Australia. A man of sentimental complications, jauntiness as became an Inniskilling, a Cockney accent such as ornaments the inhabitants of Sydney, and a complete distrust of lawyers. On the other hand, with the completest trust in Tietjens. Over his shoulder—he was blond, upright, with his numerals shining like gold, looked a lumpish, *café-au-lait*, eagle-nosed countenance: a half-caste member of one of the Six Nations, who had been a doctor's errand boy in Quebec. . . . He had his troubles, but was difficult to understand. Behind him, very black-avised with a high colour, truculent eyes, and an Irish accent, was a graduate of McGill University who had been a teacher of languages in Tokyo and had some sort of claim against the Japanese Government. . . . And faces, two and two, in a coil round the hut . . . like dust, like a cloud of dust that would approach and overwhelm a landscape; every one with preposterous troubles and anxieties, even if they did not overwhelm you personally with them . . . Brown dust. . . . (*NMP*, p. 319).

Reason here has already begun to organize what it sees. Tietjens ranges the men, one after the other, in categories. But the sheer number of his categories, and of his subcategories, since the men do not, so to speak, run true to form—the Canadian has served in the Inniskillings and owned cows in Sydney, the Irish graduate of McGill has financial difficulties in Tokyo—suggests that the world requires an infinity of intellectual divisions. And even then, even if reason could weave its net of distinctions infinitely fine, the world would still elude its grip. Like the waves and like dust, the men and their affairs are apparently numberless and in a continual process of change.

While the evidence of perception may baffle the perceiver by its very abundance, Ford shows that it may also frustrate him by its insufficiency. The mind that focuses on a large area of the world may find too much to comprehend, but the mind that approaches a single problem or group of problems may find too little. At the beginning of *A Man Could Stand Up—*, for example, Valentine receives a telephone call at the moment of the Armistice. Amid the noise of sirens and cheers, she hears no more than fragments of a message spoken by a voice that is only vaguely familiar:

". . . that he ought presumably to be under control, which you mightn't like!"

"His brothers.s.s got pneumonia, so his mistress.ss.ss even is unavailable to look after . . ."

"They're said to be friends now!"

[After inquiring the identity of the speaker.] She got back a title. . . . Lady someone or other. . . . It might have been Blastus.

"The porter said he had no furniture at all. . . . He did not appear to recognise the porter. . . ." (*MCSU*, pp. 503-505)

The fragments have little logical relationship and no logical sequence. They comprise a mixture of the apparently important and the apparently trivial. Throughout Part One of *A Man Could Stand Up—*, Valentine, as well she might, runs over and over them in an effort to grasp their significance. They represent, as it were, a close-up of one of the men on Tietjens' list—but a close-up that is perplexingly indistinct.

Both patterns of evidence, the superabundant and the insufficient, reflect from different vantage points the same external world. And both signify that that world is disinclined to cooperate with those who would understand it. Indeed, Ford sums up the recalcitrance of experience in a single symbolic metaphor. "The orderly hands you a dishevelled mass of faintly typewritten matter, thumbed out of all chance of legibility, with the orders for November 16 fastened inextricably into the middle of those for the 1st of December, and those for the 10th, 15th, and 29th missing altogether . . ." (*NMP*, p. 341). The thought is Tietjens', as he compares Sylvia's baffling actions to battalion orders. But his metaphor may clearly be given a wider application.

Ford also shows the mind not only listing and categorizing evidence but trying to transform it into a system of knowledge— about the natural world, about individuals, about itself. To pursue Tietjens' metaphor, the mind attempts to read the "faintly typewritten matter" and to imagine the import of its missing leaves. Among the second group of his patterns of thought is inference.

Only *Parade's End* itself can show the frequency with which this pattern occurs, but a few excerpts can illustrate its nature.

Why, Tietjens asks himself in Chapter III of Part One of *No More Parades*, has Sylvia come to Rouen? And he suggests an answer:

> Until that afternoon, he had imagined that his wife, too, would rather be dead than have her affairs canvassed by the other ranks. But that assumption had to be gone over. Revised . . . Of course he might say she had gone mad. But, if he said she had gone mad he would have to revise a great deal of their relationships, so it would be as broad as it was long . . . (*NMP*, p. 342).

Madness is a possible explanation of Sylvia's action. But, initially at least, it is an explanation that entails too many others. Tietjens writes down the history of his marriage "in exact language, as if he were making a report for the use of garrison headquarters" (*NMP*, p. 345). He reminds himself that the "facts of the story *must* be stated before the moral" (*NMP*, p. 345), then he turns to consider other and more likely reasons for Sylvia's arrival:

> What in the world had gone wrong with Sylvia? She was giving away her own game, and that he had never known her do. But she could not have made more certain, if she had wanted to, of returning him to his allegiance to Miss Wannop than by forcing herself there into his private life and doing it with such blatant vulgarity. For what she had done had been to make scenes before the servants! All the while he had been in France she had been working up to it. Now she had done it, before the Tommies of his own unit. But Sylvia did not make mistakes like that. It was a game. What game? He didn't even attempt to conjecture! She could not expect that he would in the future even extend to her the shelter of his roof. . . . What then was the game? (*NMP*, p. 350)

Here, indeed, Tietjens makes some small progress. On the basis of past experience, he can conclude that, provided she is sane, Sylvia has come to Rouen for a purpose. But then he must ask: what purpose? And he cannot answer. His chain of inference begins and ends with a question.

Tietjens' impasse may be due in part to the nature of experience. Sylvia's motives are complex and her game accordingly intricate.

But *No More Parades* answers the question. Sylvia has come to Rouen to seduce Tietjens. Or rather, she has come to fail to seduce him under the most dramatic and damaging circumstances. And the novel as a whole suggests that the breakdown of Tietjens' inquiry, his failure firmly to connect the fact of Sylvia's arrival with the fact of her passion for him, may be, again in part, his own fault. The nature of experience is one impediment to knowledge. The mind itself may be another.

The characters in *Parade's End* not only try to systematize the material of perception; they try to systematize it along certain preconceived lines. Or, in the language of logic, the mind as Ford creates it shows a decided preference for deductive reasoning. The individual owns a copious stock of major premises—the fruit sometimes of his own inductive labor, but more often simply a legacy from tradition. And to these premises he is only too ready to fit what he sees and hears. When Sylvia tells General Campion that Tietjens is a Socialist, for example, the General reasons aloud in the following manner:

> "Of course, refusing property is a sign of being one of these fellows. By Jove, I must go. . . . But as for his not going to live at Groby. . . . If he is setting up house with Miss Wannop. . . . Well, he could not flaunt her in the face of the county. . . . And, of course, those sheets! . . . As you put it it looked as if he'd beggared himself with his dissipations. . . . But of course, if he is refusing money from Mark, it's another matter. . . . Mark would make up a couple of hundred dozen pairs of sheets without turning a hair. . . . Of course there are the extraordinary things Christopher says. I've often heard you complain of the immoral way he looks at the serious affairs of life. . . . You said he once talked of lethal-chambering unfit children" (*NMP*, pp. 411-412).

The General is in a muddle. So much is immediately and humorously plain. But there is more in the passage than meets the casual eye. (Since the General reasons elliptically, I shall have to flesh the bones of his speech. Doubtless different readers would round out his propositions in somewhat different ways. Nonetheless, the care with which Ford elsewhere elaborates the traditional code lends at least some authority to my proceeding. The experience of the tetralogy as a whole makes it fairly easy to think as Campion and his gentlemanly colleagues think.)

At once, the General is disposed to credit Sylvia's statement. He tacitly supplies a major premise, measures a fact against it, and reaches a conclusion:

> Socialists refuse to inherit ancestral estates.
> Tietjens refuses to inherit Groby.
> ∴. Tietjens is a Socialist.

Then, however, the General remembers a conflicting piece of evidence. He seems, albeit dimly, aware that his first conclusion would be valid only if his major premise read: only Socialists refuse property. He runs through a second deductive syllogism:

> Gentlemen do not live in ancestral mansions with mistresses of good family.
> Tietjens is going to live with his mistress, Valentine.
> ∴. Tietjens refuses Groby because he is going to live with Valentine.

Tietjens, then, may not be a Socialist, since he has another reason for refusing Groby. For the moment, the General stops to consolidate this position. He tries to substantiate part of his foregoing minor premise—Tietjens has taken Valentine as his mistress—with two further deductions:

> Gentlemen do not steal unless they have beggared themselves.
> Tietjens has stolen (specifically, two pairs of Sylvia's best sheets).
> ∴. Tietjens has beggared himself.

> Gentlemen beggar themselves for just three reasons: drinking, betting, and women.
> Tietjens has not beggared himself with drinking or betting.
> ∴. Tietjens has beggared himself for women (specifically, for Valentine).

But, once again, the General recalls further evidence. He reverses the gears of his logic and returns to his first conclusion (it would not, perhaps, be unfair to infer that he now posits a restrictive major premise):

> Only Socialists refuse money.

> Tietjens refuses money.
> ∴ Tietjens is a Socialist.

By way of corroboration, he supplies a second syllogism with the same conclusion:

> Only Socialists have immoral views.
> Tietjens has immoral views.
> ∴ Tietjens is a Socialist.

And he confirms his minor premise with a further deduction:

> That unfit children should be lethal-chambered is an immoral view.
> Tietjens holds that view.
> ∴ Tietjens holds an immoral view.

Presumably, the General here makes his one attempt at induction. He jumps fast and far from view to views: Tietjens has immoral views.

The General's intellectual powers are open, wide open it seems, to criticism. As the narrative voice notes at one point, General Campion does not like to engage in arguments because he usually loses them. Yet the same voice also allows that the General is a good soldier. He is, specifically, good at logistics and good at tactics. In some ways, then, his mind is able enough; and the nature of his intellectual strength and weakness is significant. Consider again his response to Sylvia's unexpected "news."

If the General's first major premise is discarded, as he himself appears to discard it, and his fifth and sixth are made restrictive, as he seems to make them, then all his conclusions are *validly* derived. They follow logically from their major and minor premises. But only one of his conclusions is *true*; only one makes an accurate statement about the external world and it makes it, as it were, by the by. Tietjens has indeed beggared himself, but the proof of his poverty appears not in the General's deductive system but elsewhere in the world of the novel. The General is at fault in his adoption of major and minor premises. His first six major premises, all general statements about the way the world is, are false. Not one will stand the test of experience. His final premise—that unfit children should be lethal-chambered is an immoral view—can neither be proved nor disproved. It does not describe the world, but expresses an ethical position and rests ultimately upon belief.

As evidence from the rest of the tetralogy will show, the General fares somewhat better with his minor premises. Suffice it to say that roughly half of them are true. But even this success seems rather fortuitous than deserved. For the most part, the General has simply relied on hearsay, and his authorities—Sandbach, Sandbach's wife Lady Claudine, and Sylvia—are notoriously unreliable.

Within the narrow horizons of his own premises, then, the General reasons fairly well. His errors proceed primarily from his failure to look abroad. Neglecting to remind himself that "the facts of the story *must* be stated before the moral," he jumps to conclusions on insufficient evidence gathered from dubious sources. It is a fault he shares with most other characters in *Parade's End*, even at times with Tietjens. Indeed, in *Some Do Not* . . . , Valentine mocks Tietjens with his preference for preconception: "[Your mind] picks up useless facts as silver after you've polished it picks up sulphur vapour; and tarnishes! It arranges the useless facts in obsolescent patterns and makes Toryism out of them. . ." (*SDN*, p. 135).

Why this persistent tendency to turn away from experience? With the recollection of Dowell's involuted narrative and of the broad thematic movements of *Parade's End*, the final answer becomes, of course, obvious enough. Sooner or later the inquiring mind must discover the vulnerability of its own assumptions. The individual must doubt his own goodness; he must even doubt his own ethical standards. Inquiry, in short, generates more uncertainty than certainty, more insecurity than safety. Yet Ford's methods are less obvious than his conclusions. And it is interesting to see him surprising, as it were, the minds of his characters in the very moment of contact with experience.

Ford is lavish in *Parade's End* with pauses and with incomplete and broken sentences. Many of these interruptions—they are common enough in stream of consciousness—simply show that the mind searches for words or switches from one idea to another or is liable to distraction by external events. But others of Ford's broken sequences have the special significance of revealing his characters in the very process of resisting reality. The mind gains the threshold of truth, pauses, and then retreats. Thus in the following passage, where she is on the point of deciding to live with Tietjens, Valentine twice breaks off her thoughts, presumably at the words "virginity" and "chaste":

> She must not read the rest of the letter. She must not be certain. If she were certain she would have no hope of preserving her . . . Of remaining . . . (*MCSU*, p. 652).

Sometimes the retreat from experience is not so thorough. After pausing, the mind summons courage sufficient to complete its thought—obliquely. It returns to the threshold and looks, not at truth but at the shadow of truth. The mind, in short, resorts to euphemism. Here is Valentine approaching once again her determination, or rather, her near-determination, to become Tietjens' mistress:

> She ought to go away; instead she had shut the door on . . . Not on Armistice Day! What was it like to be . . . changed! (*MCSU*, p. 647)

And in the halting speech of Miss Wanostrocht, the product of late Victorian Oxford, Ford carries the process of hesitation and evasion to a still further extreme. Below, Miss Wanostrocht tries to tell Valentine how to manage her students on Armistice morning:

> "The idea is, Miss Wannop, that They should be kept—that you should keep them, please—as nearly as possible—isn't it called?—at attention until the—eh—noises . . . announce the . . . well, *you* know" (*MCSU*, p. 511).

Closely akin to the pattern of interruption—indeed just one further degree in courage removed from it—are various patterns of adverbial stress. The following quotations (in which the italics are mine) are taken from sequences of thought; they represent, that is, not narrative comment but characters' reactions to events:

> He [McKechnie] hissed—he *really* hissed because he was trying to speak under his breath (*MCSU*, p. 573).

> He [Tietjens] was leaning down, *positively*, as if over a very distinguished, elderly, seated lady (*MCSU*, p. 657).

> She [Mrs. Macmaster] had *actually* visited Sylvia in order to see

if Sylvia would not use her influence with Christopher (*LP*, p. 787).

Here the mind does look straight at reality, but it still reveals signs of resistance to it. The thinker registers astonishment and at the same time he works to convince himself that what he apprehends as true is indeed true.

Adverbial stress is one counter to incredulity. Repetition is another. In the following passage, Valentine succeeds in realizing just one of the consequences of November 11:

> People would be able to travel now. It was incredible! Incredible! Incredible! But you *could*. Next week you would be able to! You could call a taxi! And go to Charing Cross! And have a porter! A whole porter! . . . (*MCSU*, p. 506)

(And here, of course, she reveals her astonishment not only by what she says but by her staccato syntactical units, her pattern of exclamation.) Patterns of repetition more extensive and more intricate than Valentine's occur throughout *Parade's End*. In the following passage, for example, Sylvia uses a combination of restatement and elaboration in order to assure herself that her perceptions are reliable:

> They promoted this beanfeast of carnage for their own ends; they caused the deaths of men in inconceivable holocausts of pain and terror. Then they had crises of agony over the death of one single man. For it was plain to her that Tietjens was in the middle of a full nervous breakdown. Over one man's death! She had never seen him so suffer; she had never seen him so appeal for sympathy—him, a cold fiend of reticence! Yet he was now in agony! Now! . . . (*NMP*, p. 438)

Her hyperbole is, like the pattern of adverbial stress, another form of emphasis, another sign of the mind's effort to overcome incredulity.

To the mind as Ford creates it, experience appears to be a continual series of sledge-hammer blows. The genesis of so much shock is certainly twofold. The complications and chaos of experience are in themselves surprising, and they are doubly so to the mind that longs for and expects to find an orderly and predictable world. So much exclamation, so much stress and repetition betoken a more or less constant reversal of expectations. Sylvia, for example, has long been accustomed to Tietjens' reticence and apparent self-sufficiency. And, although she is aware of the paradox of her own kindness and cruelty, she has always assumed that her "enemies," Tietjens and other traditional men, are reasonable and consistent human beings. Then, in a single moment of insight, she sees Tietjens in agony over an event that he himself, as an upholder of tradition, has sanctioned. Had she not had expectations to the contrary, Sylvia would not be so astonished.

To experience—to the external world that the mind perceives—belongs, in part, the self. In *Parade's End* Ford's characters come, of course, to a variety of startling realizations. Sylvia realizes, for example, that she is one of the crowd in Rouen. Her insight rests on a sudden apprehension of similarities. Already aware of her own chaos, she suddenly realizes the chaotic nature of the society in which she finds herself and makes an immediate connection: she and society both tend toward destruction. Hers is a common mode of intellection, the method of the scientist and the historian. But there are moments in *Parade's End* of more primitive, or earlier, realization—as if Ford were creating Sylvia not only in the process of grasping the nature of the crowd and her connection with it, but in the very process of learning that she and the crowd exist.

The self suddenly surprises the self in the midst of various emotions or actions. And the conscious mind becomes aware that it is linked to an unconscious that harbors predilections and issues effective orders. It is this kind of realization that we know Tietjens experiences from the sentence, "He was leaning down, positively, as if over a very distinguished, elderly, seated lady." He has caught himself, as he speaks to Valentine's mother over the telephone, in an unconscious act of gentlemanly deference. He has discovered in himself a disposition to fulfill the old rituals of tradition at the very moment when he intends to break with them, by living with Valentine. Again and again in *Parade's End*, Tietjens and his fellows record, with exclamation, stress, and repetition, the astonishing emergence of the subconscious into the conscious.

In many ways the world of *Parade's End* is grim enough to satisfy the disillusioned or even the cynical. But there are limits to Ford's pessimism. While his characters face much that is painful, they also meet much that is joyful. Yet so tenacious is their hold on the familiar, even when the familiar is unpleasant, that they have to convince themselves that they can be, or even that they are, happy. Thus Valentine, used to war, is astonished at the Armistice. She has to overcome her resistance to that news and all its implications. In the same way, she must bring herself to believe that Tietjens loves her—loves her and has come back from the war to live with her. Since they are all adept at evasion, Ford's characters cannot complain that the world is too much *with* them, but they can and do complain that it is too much *for* them.

With the exception of interruption, all Ford's patterns of thought that emphasize mind rather than experience combine to form a pattern of their own. Induction and deduction are ways of proving; and exclamation, stress, repetition, and restatement are ways of persuading. It would be an exaggeration to say that Ford's characters feel obliged to convince themselves, or their listeners, of every observation they make. But it is true that, compared with the characters of other novelists and compared with most people in real life, they feel obliged to underline and substantiate an extraordinary number of their perceptions and statements.

The disposition to convince is even more evident in conversation than in sequences of thought. Ford's characters seldom speak coolly. Fresh from the blows of experience, they speak under the pressure of emotion and they seek to communicate that emotion. They also assume that their audience is hostile to their ideas or, at the very best, indifferent. They expect to find their own resistance to enlightenment shared by their listeners and they strive, sometimes desperately, to combat it. "Conversation" is really too mild a word for most of Ford's spoken discourse. His characters seldom talk to exchange amenities, seldom even to inform. Typically, they emphasize, they insist, they seek to overwhelm opposition. And if they are reluctant to gather data, they are more than liberal in the use of data they already possess. Here, for example, is Valentine Wannop addressing Tietjens during their second meeting:

> "It's obvious mother means us to see a great deal of you. *You're* going to be a mascot too, like your father. I suppose you think you are: you saved me from the police yesterday, you appear to have saved mother's neck to-day. You appear, too, to be going to

make twenty pounds profit on a horse deal. You say you will and you seem to be that sort of a person . . . Twenty pounds is no end in a family like ours . . . Well, then, you appear to be going to be the regular *bel ami* of the Wannop family . . ." (*SDN*, p. 113)

Valentine voices a general statement, backs it to the hilt with evidence, and then repeats it. The very existence of her argument and the length of her chain of proof suggest that she speaks not so much to prove that Tietjens is going to be a family friend as to disprove an assumption to the contrary. She speaks as if she has been challenged, but the first glove on the ground is her own. *After* she finishes her speech, Tietjens says quietly, "I hope not." Whether Valentine anticipates his response or causes it remains, perhaps, debatable.

Even when the situation offers no suggestion whatsoever of external challenge, Ford's characters are apt to assume opposition. In the following address to Tietjens, Mrs. Wannop finishes by explicitly adopting a defensive posture. She suspects Tietjens of having objections he never makes:

"Of course, I back my daughter against the cats and monkeys. Of course, I back Valentine through thick and thin. I'd back her if she lived with a married man or had illegitimate children. But I don't approve, I don't approve of the suffragettes: I despise their aims, I detest their methods. I don't think young girls ought to talk to strange men. Valentine spoke to you and look at the worry it has caused you. I disapprove. I'm a woman, but I've made my own way: other women could do it if they liked or had the energy. I disapprove! But don't believe that I will ever go back on any suffragette, individual, in gangs; my Valentine or any other. Don't believe that I will ever say a word against them that's to be repeated—*you* won't repeat them. Or that I will ever write a word against them. No, I'm a woman and I stand by my sex!" (*SDN*, p. 123)

Mrs. Wannop has at her disposal the makings of a decent argument. To be reasonable, she has merely to subordinate one of her two main points to the other: "Although I disapprove of the suffragettes, I am, above all, loyal to my own sex"; or, the other way round, "Although I am loyal to women, my loyalty stops short of sanctioning the methods and aims of the suffragettes." But she is unwilling to make any final concession. And she is clearly uncomfortable. She restates the points of her argument again and again and again. Beneath the smoke of so much convincing burns, of course, the fire not of certainty but of doubt. Even in spoken discourse the ultimate opponent sometimes appears to be not the listener but the speaker himself.

While Ford's characters argue strenuously, their arguments are, more often than not, without visible consequence in the world of *Parade's End*. They frequently fail to listen to one another. At times, they scarcely listen to themselves. Thus Sylvia admits to Father Consett that her career of adultery must be short-lived and unhappy, emphasizing her admission with detail and repetition. Yet in the end her argument counts for nothing. What she presents convincingly—what she "knows" and "believes"—has no influence on her final attitude:

> "The catalogue of the defects of age; I know them. One grows skinny—my sort—the complexion fades, the teeth stick out. And then there is the boredom. I know it; one is bored . . . bored . . . bored! You can't tell me anything I don't know about that. I'm thirty. I know what to expect. You'd like to have told me, Father, only you were afraid of taking away from your famous man of the world effect—you'd like to have told me that one can insure against the boredom and the long, skinny teeth by love of husband and child. The home stunt! I believe it! I do quite believe it. Only I hate my husband . . . and I hate . . . I hate my child" (*SDN*, p. 38).

The motions of convincing, and of proving, become even more obviously detached from their usual ends in the following speech of General Campion's. It records the general's first response to the "news" that Tietjens is a Socialist:

> "Christopher! . . . A So . . ." He gasped as if he could not pronounce the word. He said: "Damn it all! . . . I've loved that boy. . . . He's my only godson. . . . His father was my best friend. . . . I've watched over him. . . . I'd have married his mother if she would have had me. . . . Damn it all, he's down in my will as residuary legatee after a few small things left to my

sister and my collection of horns to the regiment I commanded. . . ." (*NMP*, p. 410)

In part, the General expresses his sense of injury. But in part also he goes through the motions of refuting Sylvia's information at the very moment that he accepts it. In the General's traditional world, certain social ties entail certain kinds of behavior. And all his pieces of evidence are, to him, reasons why Tietjens should not be, virtually cannot be, a Socialist. The "proving mechanism" operates independently, automatically, after the mind has already discounted its efforts.

In his paragraphs, his sentences, even his phrases, Ford presents reason as a poor and inadequate instrument. The mind, to be sure, is capable of logic. But logic alone cannot determine truth. The world resists interpretation; more importantly, the mind with its need for security resists the world. It may even resist the force of its own arguments. *Parade's End* is a tragicomedy of errors in a very specific and detailed way.

At times, in *Parade's End*, characters deliberately employ false premises as a means to unscrupulous ends. Tietjens reckons French materiel losses solely on the basis of damage to bricks and mortar, and Macmaster wins a knighthood by submitting the gross underestimate to his government. Tietjens himself, with a series of half-truths, repeatedly guides Rugely, General Campion, and other gentlemen to false conclusions about his marriage. But reason in *Parade's End* is more often blind than Machiavellian. Most mistakes are sincere, in the sense that the conscious mind does not will them and recognizes them, if at all, only after they are made.

The players of the traditional game wander in a no man's land between appearance and reality. Their premises ultimately spring, of course, from their contrary passions and aspirations. Yet once a system is erected on an incomplete understanding of human nature or a corrupt conception of virtue, it takes on a life of its own and perpetuates error. In the Boer War General Campion uselessly sacrificed half a company because he had false intelligence. In a similar way, the adherents of tradition injure themselves and one another because they accept misleading information about what should be and what is. Ford does not precisely apportion the blame for injury between human desire, whether for anarchy or impossible goodness, and human reason. Nor does he need to. The point is that both causes may work together to bad ends. The clouds of gossip that attend Tietjens' erratic career are formed by error as well as malice. Tietjens himself is doubly responsible for Perowne's appearance at the door of Sylvia's bedroom in Rouen. He has ordered his marriage sometimes by principles of tradition, sometimes by those of saintliness, and he has overlooked the very obvious fact that his discipline has all the while aggravated Sylvia's tendency to destruction. His pride has been intellectual as well as spiritual. He has, indeed, made errors in judgment.

With the death of tradition, Ford cannot credibly restore the minds of his characters to a state of primitive innocence. And yet in the third volume of his tetralogy he manages to achieve something very like that. Historically, the first world war destroyed neither the English ruling class nor its attitudes. The process of dissolution continued for some years after November 11, 1918, and it still continues. In *Parade's End*, however, Ford uses the artist's license to hasten historical development. In *A Man Could Stand Up—*, he narrows his focus to Valentine and Tietjens and shows them both in the ruins of traditional society. For all their faults of intellect, Valentine hearing the tumult of the Armistice in London and Tietjens listening to German shells over France know that *their* civilization has spent itself. While they are not suddenly released from the premises of the past, they are suddenly placed in situations where those premises are no longer relevant. For all practical purposes, their minds are as clean as *tabulae rasae*— although their "state of nature" is terrible rather than benign.

Part One of *A Man Could Stand Up—* is primarily an overture to Part Two. Although Valentine's experiences in London are chronologically later than Tietjens' in France, they introduce themes that the time shift backward takes up and carries to full development. It is in Part Two, then, that Ford carries to its furthest extreme the inner chaos that attends the loss of tradition. The burden of his realization—it is a picture of near-insanity—he carries mainly through the elaboration of certain of his familiar patterns of thought. But he accompanies his inner drama with a counterpoint of symbolic landscape and incident. Since Part Two covers nearly 200 pages, I shall restrict my account mainly to Chapter I and focus even more narrowly on the end of that chapter, which presents a series of shifts to a still earlier time.

Chapter I discovers Tietjens waiting at dawn for a German artillery bombardment. Twice during the night he has sent runners back to his own base with a request for Mills bombs. He has received no reply and wonders: "Who knew if there was anyone in charge there?" (*MCSU*, p. 544) The intentions of base headquarters are as obscure as those of the opposing Germans. The coming bombardment might be the usual morning event. Or it might be the rumored Great Strafe, herald of a major enemy attack. Even the situation on his own front line is matter for speculation, since Tietjens learns that his battalion has lost contact with its flanking Allies.

Physically isolated, Tietjens is also isolated from precedent. The illness of his C.O. has precipitated him into a command for which he has no experience. He does not know "what he ought to do by the book" (*MCSU*, p. 576); and even if he did, there are ample indications that the old routine of the traditional army is obsolete. His battalion is only at one-third strength and, though still the Glamorganshires in name, its men are mainly replacements from Derby. An "extraordinary Falstaff's battalion of muddy odd-come shorts" (*MCSU*, p. 571), hastily and badly trained, they are not familiar with gentlemen's rules of war. They are not even familiar with gentlemen. And the most recent status quo of warfare is in danger of being overturned. If the Great Strafe and the attack materialize, Tietjens and his men will have to fall back quickly. They will have to fight a mobile war for which they are totally unprepared. Tietjens, then, is everywhere confronted by the unknown and can only improvise.

As relentlessly as he isolates Tietjens' military position, Ford turns his hero's mind in upon itself. The chapter begins with a significant wish:

> Months and months before Christopher Tietjens had stood extremely wishing that his head were level with a particular splash of purposeless whitewash. Something behind his mind forced him to the conviction that, if his head—and of course the rest of his trunk and lower limbs—were suspended by a process of levitation to that distance above the duckboard on

which, now, his feet were, he would be in an inviolable sphere (*MCSU*, p. 543).

Tietjens quickly tags the wish—it is really an obsession—irrational. But he cannot control it. It returns again and again to his consciousness. The worst of his ordeal under fire will be his mind's capacity to attend on its own disorders.

The obsession is only one of a number of simultaneous mental activities. Tietjens questions his men, issues orders, trains his field glasses on no man's land, wets his finger and feels the wind. He remembers the past and, above all, tries to read the meaning of what he presently sees and hears. These activities at first seem natural enough, but it quickly becomes apparent that some of them, his memories and his inferences particularly, take an unnatural turn.

The present reminds him only of his very recent and his very distant past. Circumstances prompt him to recollect much about his army experience, but from his previous personal life he recalls only a few details about his childhood and his childhood home. He remembers old cannons he saw as a child, remembers also autumn mornings and the moors above Groby, and the sound of picks going in the Yorkshire mines. This closure of the springs of memory, unlike the amnesia Tietjens suffers earlier, in *Some Do Not. . .* , has no physical cause. It signifies, rather, the extent to which his situation at the front has detached him from his familiar world.

Cut off from most of the past and most sources of information in the present, Tietjens' speculations proceed virtually unchecked. He scrutinizes the limited data at his disposal; he even scrutinizes the symbols for those data. With a scrupulosity appropriate only to the scholar in his study, he begins to question the very words with which he thinks. And he ends by dissociating himself further still from the familiar:

> It was more descriptive to call what had spoken a cannon than a gun—though it was not done in the best local circles. It was all right to call 75's or the implements of the horse artillery "guns"; they were mobile and toy-like. But those immense things were cannons; the sullen muzzles always elevated. [. . .]

Cannon. . . . Yes, that was the right thing to call them (*MCSU,* pp. 544-545).

As far as one could tell three salvoes of a dozen shells each at half-minute intervals between the salvoes. Perhaps salvoes was not the right word (*MCSU,* p. 545).

[The Germans] held their front lines always very sparsely. . . . Was that the phrase? Was it even English? (*MCSU,* p. 549)

At the same time, training his glasses on no man's land, Tietjens constructs a strange and frightening scene. He sees "shadows, like the corrugations of photographs of the moon" (*MCSU,* p. 549). He thinks, for a moment, that a number of wet trenching sacks are men "creeping up" (*MCSU,* p. 549). And he transforms the mists above the German lines into gigantic specters. "They mopped and mowed, fantastically; grey, with black shadows; dropping like the dishevelled veils of murdered bodies. They were engaged in fantastic and horrifying laying out of corpses of vast dimensions; in silence, but in accord, they performed unthinkable tasks" (*MCSU,* p. 550). Clearly, Tietjens has begun to cross the boundary between perception and hallucination.

Through a series of time shifts Ford gathers his several themes of inner chaos to a climax. He takes us back to a previous bombardment and attack: Tietjens is lying in his sleeping bag in a wine cellar, speculating on the Germans' motives. Why, he wonders, did they launch the attack he has just witnessed? And he provides a number of answers, each one outlining a larger and more complicated strategy than the last:

They had sent over that thin waft of men under a blessed lot of barrage and stuff. . . . A lot! A *whole* lot! It had been really quite an artillery *strafe.* Ten thousand shells as like as not. Then, somewhere up the line they had probably made a demonstration in force. *Great* bodies of men, an immense surge. And twenty to thirty thousand shells. Very likely some miles of esplanade, as it were, with the sea battering against it. And only a demonstration in force. . . .

It could not be real fighting. They had not been ready for their spring advance.

It had been meant to impress somebody imbecile. . . . Somebody imbecile in Wallachia, or Sofia, or Asia Minor. Or Whitehall, very likely. Or the White House! [. . .] Or, of course, our own legislators might have been trying a nice little demonstration in force, equally idiotic somewhere else, to impress someone just as unlikely to be impressed. . . . This, then, would be the answer! (*MCSU*, pp. 562-563).

The pattern here, of course, is inference. But it is inference running wild, building a skyscraper of surmise on a ludicrously shallow basis of fact.

At intervals, moreover, the present intrudes and prompts further speculation. Tietjens hears picks digging beneath his cellar, then the words *"Bringt dem Hauptmann eine Kerze!"* He begins to imagine the Germans: "It was, of course, just like German spooks to go mining by candle-light. Obsoletely Nibelungen-like. Dwarfs probably!" (*MCSU*, p. 562). And he turns his power of reason on his imaginary picture—not, however, to question the picture itself, but only one of its minute details: "He imagined that the Hauptmann spark must be myopic; short-sightedly examining a tamping fuse. . . . If they used tamping fuses or if that was what they called them in the army!" (*MCSU*, p. 563) Before the end of Chapter I, Tietjens has inferred that the enemy attack might just as well have originated in Whitehall as Unter den Linden. And he has transformed the Germans of his imagination into primitive and terrifying beings:

> They were packed in the tunnel; whitish-grey, tubular agglomerations. . . . Large! Like the maggots that are eaten by Australian natives. . . . Fear possessed him!
>
> He sat up in his flea-bag, dripping with icy sweat.
>
> "By jove, I'm for it!" he said. He imagined that his brain was going; he was mad and seeing himself go mad. He cast about in his mind for some subject about which to think so that he could prove to himself that he had not gone mad (*MCSU*, pp. 563-564).

Ford has foreshadowed the form of Tietjens' near-insanity in his treatment of McKechnie, of Sylvia, and of Valentine. In one of his recurrent moments of madness, McKechnie says, "Our headquarters are full of Huns doing the Huns' work" (*NMP*, p. 304). At other moments of unreason, he blames his misfortunes on other "enemies," his uncle Macmaster or Tietjens. In Rouen,

Sylvia thinks the Virgin Mary has "given it [her] in the neck" and she wonders if she must war with heaven. Although Valentine explicitly accuses no natural or supernatural powers of malevolence, she exaggerates the wrongs she believes society in general and her father in particular have done her. With its passion for certainty, the mind as Ford creates it tends to construct design where no design exists. And in moments of strain and misfortune, the mind tends to construct a malevolent picture of the world—reading, in short, a routine German attack as evidence of wholesale betrayal in Whitehall.

With that "conclusion," however, Tietjens reaches the crisis of his internal chaos. Indeed, almost imperceptibly, the process of recovery has already begun. The crisis occurs, significantly, in the past. And during the course of it Tietjens has recalled a saving memory, the name Valentine. With the return to the present, he begins to remember other parts of his past and regains command of his mind.

Tietjens also begins to construct a new way of life. He can scarcely remember Valentine's face, but he remembers her mind very well:

> It was the mentality that obsessed him: the exact mind, the impatience of solecisms and facile generalisations! [. . .] She was, in effect, the only person in the world that he wanted to hear speak. Certainly the only person in the world that he wanted to talk to. The only clear intelligence! . . . The repose that his mind needed from the crackling of thorns under all the pots of the world . . . (*MCSU*, p. 604).

Although he rejects the ideals both of saintliness and tradition, Tietjens cannot exorcise his longing for intellectual certainty. There is, perhaps, a hint here that reason may some time help him to order and evaluate his world. But life cannot wait for the outcome of "infinite [. . .] communings" (*MCSU*, p. 635). And, for the urgent present, the soundest conclusion that reason can reach is that reason itself is inadequate to solve ethical problems. While *Parade's End* is an intellectual work, its ultimate values are almost wholly anti-intellectual.

The bases of Tietjens' new life are emotion and hard work. Love alone prompts and justifies his union with Valentine. The implication, supported by the tetralogy as a whole, is this: if he and Valentine express their "quite ordinary" natures (*MCSU*, p. 622), if they forego the temptation to transform their humanity into something finer, then they will not risk changing it into something baser. They will steer between the Scylla and Charybdis of repression and lawlessness. With its dismissal of intellect and its reliance on emotion or instinct, *A Man Could Stand Up*— might easily have been (like *The 'Half Moon'*) both facile and sentimental. But Tietjens and Valentine are tried and tempered by experience. Their reunion, conducted in understatement against a setting of bare walls, is by its very nature controlled. And Ford never suggests that love leads them to live quite happily ever after. They remember the war and its losses. They have in *The Last Post* their wholly plausible and painful domestic differences.

The hard work Ford presents in *Parade's End*, with manifest affection as well as approval, is of two kinds. A soldier who loads his rifle under fire with drill-movements, another who fires Verey lights at regular intervals, Valentine jumping in a way that is "perfectly business-like" (*SDN*, p. 68), Tietjens handling horses, rigging vertical drains, buying antiques—all represent an ideal of nonintellectual endeavor. They exert their "bread-and-butter brains" (*MCSU*, p. 526) to accomplish relatively simple and wholly useful tasks. They discipline the body, or else they manipulate things rather than ideas. In *The New Humpty-Dumpty* Ford satirized the William Morris movement, and in his memoirs he ridiculed his own youthful allegiance to it. In *Parade's End* he scores the Pre-Raphaelite affectations of Mrs. Duchemin, with her long silk sleeves and amber beads, but he remains loyal to the principle of craftsmanship.

The other kind of work, to which Ford gives considerably less emphasis, is—and this is its virtue—wholly intellectual. The seventeenth-century poems that Tietjens recalls in *A Man Could Stand Up*— are "exact and quiet" (*MCSU*, p. 564). And figures are "clean" (*MCSU*, p. 549). In the abstract realms of its own creation, though not in human affairs, reason may operate flawlessly and legitimately, and it may for a time solace its need for certainty. Figures are also "comforting" things (*MCSU*, p. 549). Indeed, both kinds of work are to a certain extent therapeutic. They are channels that draw away energy that might otherwise result in emotional or mental disorder.

The Last Post restates the death of tradition and confirms the new values of *A Man Could Stand Up—*. Although it is a full-length novel rather than a scene, it is, like the description of Edward Ashburnham's suicide, a recapitulation or coda.[11]

In the last novel of his tetralogy, Ford creates a pastoral world, neither wholly real nor ideal. Its setting, to be sure, is authentic, from the chickens "scream[ing] with the voice of poultry disaster" (*LP*, p. 696) to the aspidistras and Wilton carpets that decorate sometime primitive cottages. Ford knew his rural England as well as Conrad knew the sea. But against his realistic scene Ford writes a narrative that is very nearly an allegory or, perhaps, very nearly a fairy tale.

With the opening paragraph, Ford sets his dominant tone, which is peaceful, relaxed, even expansive:

> He lay staring at the withy binders of his thatch shelter; the grass was infinitely green; his view embraced four counties; the roof was supported by six small oak sapling-trunks, roughly trimmed and brushed from above by apple boughs. French crab apple! The hut had no sides (*LP*, p. 677).

The mood is broken by the intrusion of the "fause thieves" alluded to in the epigraph (*LP*, p. 675): the remnants of tradition— Campion, Sylvia, Christopher's son Mark, their host Fittleworth, Mrs. Duchemin—and the successors to tradition—the American Mrs. Millicent de Bray Pape and, in his guise of Cambridge Marxist-Communist, young Mark Tietjens again. Yet the return of calm is forecast in the fact that Ford formalizes the terms and the protagonists of his conflict.

---

11. John A. Meixner has argued that *The Last Post* should not properly be regarded as part of *Parade's End* (*Ford Madox Ford's Novels*, pp. 217-221). Ford himself appears to have opened the way to such a discussion by saying both that he did and did not intend to write a fourth volume in his Tietjens series. The vexing question of intention apart, however, continuity of character and theme alone, it seems to me, requires the inclusion of *The Last Post* in *Parade's End*. What Ford, in fact, wrote was a tetralogy, although, granted, one that is uneven.

The intruders, whom Ford first describes from the point of view of the native country people, are something less, something more than human:

A number of members of the Quality, on shining horses, their leathers creaking beautifully, rode at a walk up the path. They were the real Quality. A fine old gentleman, thin as a lath, clean face, hooky nose, white moustache, lovely cane, lovely leggings. On 'Is Lordship's favourite hack. A bay mare. A fine lady, slim as a boy, riding astride as they do to-day though they did not use to. [. . .] A boy, eighteen, maybe. Shiny leggings too: all their clothes is shiny (*LP*, p. 708).

These characters inhabit two planes of existence. There is the Sylvia who worries through the strategy of her game of torment; there is also the fine lady who looks down at Tietjens' cottage with a smile and contemplates the tiara and white dress she may some day wear in India if she divorces Tietjens and marries General Campion.

Tradition itself Ford gathers into a single symbol—Groby, the Tietjens ancestral mansion, with its walls undermined and shadowed by Groby Great Tree. Tree and mansion tumble down together under the quixotic zeal of Mrs. de Bray Pape, self-elected successor to the Maintenon, apostle of sanitation, and "the most active woman from here to Santa Fe" (*LP*, p. 718). The struggle is remote not only in time and place—the tree, it develops, is *already* down in Yorkshire—but by virtue of the symbolic simplification and the droll eccentricity of Mrs. de Bray Pape. Tietjens is still sentimentally attached to tradition, but his renunciation of it is not seriously menaced. At the end of the novel, he returns from a visit to Groby grieved at the damage he found there but doggedly faithful to Valentine and their new way of life.[12]

Part of the fairy tale, too, is Ford's continued, and now broadly humorous, criticism of reason. The opening chapters discover Mark

---

12. This is Tietjens' only appearance on stage. For the rest, he is presented indirectly in *The Last Post*, through the eyes of other characters, particularly through Mark's eyes. I think it very probable that Ford was more at ease writing "negatively," from the point of view of Mark the unregenerate traditional man, than he would have been writing "positively," from the point of view of a reconstructed hero.

Tietjens and his French wife, Marie Léonie, enjoying a communion so complete that words are unnecessary to it. Mark *will* not speak and Marie Léonie speaks endlessly, without receiving any response. Her understanding of Mark—she alone knows that he is willfully silent—rests entirely upon intuition. Craftsmen also achieve a communion virtually wordless. It is "nothing" that Marie Léonie "obstinately" speaks French to Gunning, the "all-round man" of the farm. "On his subjects he could tell by intuition what her answers to his questions were." And she can interpret his dialect "well enough" for moistening eggs, for bottling cider (*LP*, p. 695). This is a timeless world, primitive and more enduring than tradition, and it is primarily occupied not with the quest for intellectual certainty but with the fulfillment of the duties of affection and with bread-and-butter work.

This world, certainly, contains a share of misunderstanding and perplexity. Here, for example, is the joint attempt of Cramp the carpenter and Betty the maid to solve the mysteries of Marie Léonie's personality and position:

> She was 'Er Ladyship, a good mark, a foreign Frenchy. That was bad. She was extraordinarily efficient about the house and garden and poultry-yard, a matter for mixed feelings. She was fair, not black-avised, a good mark; she was buxom, not skinny, like the real Quality. A bad mark because she was, then, not real Quality; but a qualifiedly good mark because if you 'as to 'ave Quality all about you in the 'ouse tis better not to 'ave real Quality. . . . (*LP*, p. 704).

The pattern of thought is that of deductive inference, complete with given premises.

Country men, like traditional ones, are not only baffled by the entrance of the unfamiliar into their lives; they prove to be outraged as well. Whoever heard, Cramp, Mrs. Cramp, the little Cramps, and their neighbors ask as they watch Marie Léonie, of bottling cider with a tube? The police, they think, should be notified. And Cramp regards as virtually irrational Tietjens' traffic in the bits and pieces of old England. Yet while they express their prejudices, the country people do not act upon them. Albeit uneasily, they finally accept the unknown. They do not call the police. They go home, and Cramp goes on repairing and polishing antiques.

Marie Léonie, for her part, speaks at length of Tietjens' and Valentine's incomprehensible aversion to the immortal works of Monsieur Casimir-Bar and to such modern improvements as the reading desk, the revolving hut, and the aeroplane. But, while she cannot understand their tastes or their way of life, she is richly tolerant of their "singular natures" (*LP*, p. 693). With Marie Léonie, indeed, Ford mocks not only the mind's attempt to evaluate experience according to given premises but intellectual activity in general. Marie Léonie's mind is "like a cupboard, stuffed, packed with the most incongruous materials, tools, vessels, and débris. Once the door was opened you never knew what would tumble out or be followed by what" (*LP*, pp. 682-683). The only discipline Marie Léonie imposes on her discourse is wholly formal rather than semantic: she always finishes with the subject with which she begins. "She might be concluding a long comment on ironclads and have to get back suddenly to custards because the door-bell rang while her maid was out, but accomplish the transition she would before she answered the bell" (*LP*, p. 683). To Mark, whose mind is usually limited in its aims (he habitually satisfies his need for intellectual order by memorizing racing data, by predicting future winners), Marie Léonie's rupture of the rules of logic is entertaining and "restful," a diversion "as foreign travel might have been" (*LP*, p. 683). For Marie Léonie, Ford implies, loyalty, intuition, and bread-and-butter brains will suffice. Apart from her discourse, she is "frugal, shrewd, astonishingly clean and healthy" (*LP*, p. 683).

For characters of larger intelligence and more sophisticated birth, community with the timeless and enduring world is not so easily achieved and, Ford implies, never completely. The major portion of *The Last Post* traces, in Mark's mind, in Sylvia's, and in Valentine's, familiar sequences of thought. Each of these characters tries to work through a series of problems: Mark to determine the truth about his father's death; Sylvia to formulate the strategy of her game; and Valentine to weigh the pros and cons of the new game that she and Tietjens have chosen to play. The mental strain they undergo is severe. Yet at the last each manages to solve his problem not by speculation, which is fruitless, but by renewed contact with ordinary experience. Mark, recalling details of his childhood life, decides that his father's death was not suicide but simply an accident. Sylvia gives up her game when she learns that Valentine expects a child—though here, of course, Ford's resolution is not convincing. Valentine hears and accepts from Mark words of folk wisdom that counsel her to remember to love and be kind for the sake of her child. Mark as he dies and, as she withdraws, Sylvia see the peace and fulfillment that Valentine and Tietjens may enjoy if only they will.

For Ford, too, then, the world came to rest upon a few very simple ideas. But his ideas were finally different from the Conradian ones that prevailed in *The Inheritors*. Like Conrad, Ford created egoistic heroes who cherished romantic and self-destructive ideals. But he also gifted his heroes, and heroines, with other instincts that, given expression, were not harmful but healing. Despite the protests of his later novels, love had no place in Conrad's true moral world; it came to be the primary value of Ford's. And if, as his treatment of tradition suggests, Ford too was deeply skeptical of the motives and achievements of public men and public institutions, he differed again from the author of *Nostromo* in his belief in the possibility of private harmony, of personal happiness. *Parade's End* is, in Ford's own way, a very moving work.

IV

It is possible to speak, quite firmly and with an abundance of proof at hand, of typical Fordian characters, situations, and emotional and moral attitudes. But what of Ford's narrative methods and his prose style? His technique is certainly more difficult to sum up than his "story" or "stories." Like the men in Tietjens' draft, the several components of his art show signs of being elusive. There are Fordian phrases and sentences, Fordian scenes and time shifts, Fordian points of view. And what unity may be imposed on *this* diversity? The answers proposed in the rest of this chapter, I had best admit straightway, are partial. They do not pretend to "cover" Ford's technique, only to suggest a few ways in which it may be defined and so distinguished from that of other novelists.

To begin with, I wish to quote a passage from *Romance*, the second novel Ford wrote with Conrad:

> [Castro] had undoubtedly been sent by the uncle across the seas to find Carlos and bring him out of Europe; there was

something romantic in that mission. He was now a dependent of the Riego family, but there were unfathomable depths in that tubby little man's past. That he had gone to Russia at the tail of the Grande Armée, one could not help believing. He had been most likely in the grand army of sutlers and camp-followers. He could talk convincingly of the cold, and of the snows and his escape. And from his allusions one could get glimpses of what he had been before and afterwards—apparently everything that was questionable in a secularly disturbed Europe; no doubt somewhat of a bandit; a guerrillero in the sixes and sevens; with the Army of the Faith near the French border, later on. There had been room and to spare for that sort of pike, in the muddy waters, during the first years of the century.[13]

The passage occurs in Part First of the novel and on the basis of external evidence alone was almost surely written by Ford.[14] But even if there were no accounts of who wrote what in *Romance*, the passage could be convincingly attributed to Ford. The narrator notes that the first of his two initial statements of fact is "undoubtedly" true. Then he tries to fathom the "unfathomable." He makes inferences and backs them with various pieces of evidence: he refers to Castro's "talk" and "allusions" and he even refers to general conditions in early nineteenth-century Europe. The narrator, in short, does not simply report Castro's past. He is self-conscious and cautious about describing his world; he evaluates what he has heard; he proves his conclusions to his reader and to himself. This is a somewhat unusual way to present the background of a minor character. It is even an unusual way to write narrative prose, and it seems to be a typically Fordian way.

Here, by way of contrast, is Conrad's rendering of virtually the same material:

---

13. Joseph Conrad and Ford Madox Hueffer, *Romance* (London: Dent, 1949), pp. 36-37.

14. According to Conrad, Ford was almost entirely responsible for writing Part First of *Romance* and he himself for Part Fourth (see G. Jean-Aubry, *Joseph Conrad: Life and Letters* [New York: Doubleday, Page, 1927] I, 168, n. 3, and *The Richard Curle Conrad Collection*, Item 51). Though Ford's statements on the division of the collaboration are inconsistent, he did at least once come close to agreeing with Conrad's testimony, in his *Joseph Conrad* (p. 220).

Such as he was—a born vagabond, *contrabandista*, spy in armed camps, sutler at the tail of the *Grande Armée* (escaped, God only knows how, from the snows of Russia), beggar, *guerillero*, bandit, sceptically murderous, draping his rags in saturnine dignity—he had ended by becoming the sinister and grotesque squire of our quixotic Carlos. There was something romantically sombre in his devotion. He disdained to turn round at the danger, because he had left his heart on the coffin as a lesser affection would have laid a wreath.[15]

Conrad's eye is on the object, not on the mind wrestling to comprehend the object. And while Conrad alludes to the mystery of Castro's background ("God only knows how"), he nonetheless allows *his* narrator to speak confidently, even authoritatively, about his world.

This is not to say that Conrad always wrote from a point of view of certainty. He created, of course, many narrators, the hero of *Romance* among them, with imperfect knowledge. He was, moreover—and this is a point worth returning to—far more willing than the author of *The Good Soldier* and *Parade's End* to close his novels with unsolved, and perhaps insoluble, problems of judgment. (It is much more difficult to define, say, Conrad's attitude toward Decoud than Ford's toward Tietjens.) Yet it is true that Conrad shows much less concern with problems of knowing *per se*. Or, to put the matter in terms of dramatic situation, Conrad's characters, in comparison with Ford's, enjoy a fairly firm relationship with their world. In the following passage from *Lord Jim*, for example, even the eternal enigmas of Jim's personality and moral status evoke no patterns of proving:

"I don't pretend I understood him. The views he let me have of himself were like those glimpses through the shifting rents in a thick fog—bits of vivid and vanishing detail, giving no connected idea of the general aspect of a country. They fed one's curiosity without satisfying it; they were no good for purposes of orientation. Upon the whole he was misleading. That's how I summed him up to myself after he left me late in the evening."[16]

15. *Romance*, p. 253.
16. *Lord Jim* (Cambridge, Mass.: Houghton, Mifflin, 1958), p. 57.

Marlow stresses the fact that his evidence is inadequate, but then he simply summarizes instead of reasoning out and justifying step by step his momentary conclusions about Jim. The eye is still mainly on the object, and the narrator, despite his admission of ignorance, is once again authoritative.

Are Ford's patterns of thought, then, distinctively his own? No single pattern is, I think, idiosyncratic; but the combination of all of them and the frequency with which they appear in his mature work seem in themselves to amount to idiosyncrasy. The patterns reveal a remarkably consistent view of experience: the world is perplexing, even deceptive, and the human personality is driven by a need, sometimes desperate, to find and to defend intellectual and moral order.

Closely related to, indeed virtually required for, the full expression of Ford's *Weltanschauung* are certain intimate points of view: in *The Good Soldier*, a first-person narrator; in *Parade's End*, extensive sequences of thought. And Ford's personal narration and thought show a distinctive quality. To look for a moment at certain recurrent signposts, the language of intellectual order or of argument—"but," "yet," "however," "on the other hand," "nonetheless," "nevertheless," "moreover," "besides," "so," "so that," "because," "since," "for," "therefore," "then," "thus"—appears very frequently in Ford's prose, appears indeed to an extent that is unusual in fiction. Ford's characters reason about their world not only in isolated patterns of inference but more or less continually. In *Parade's End*, much of the spoken discourse even is, in Ford's way, "interior." The speaker, that is, ostensibly addresses an audience but seems really to reason aloud or to conduct a debate with himself.

But Ford's characters do not, of course, reason merely about abstractions. Ford casts much of his action within a general framework of reasoning or argument. Dowell introduces Leonora's unhappy attempt to take a lover as a contrast to her county family appearance: "I swear to you that they were the model couple. [. . .] And yet, only this afternoon, talking over the whole matter, she said to me: 'Once I tried to have a lover but I was so sick at the heart, so utterly worn out, that I had to send him away'" (pp. 8-9). The whole excursion to M—— is introduced as a "rather extraordinary instance" (p. 37) of the fact that good manners prevent intimate acquaintance. Similarly, in *No More Parades* Tietjens recalls his last meeting with Sylvia, early in the morning of his second departure to France, as he tries to reason out his wife's motives and to decide whether he is or is not morally bound to her. The whole sequence of events—Sylvia sitting quietly on the other side of the room, then raging at Tietjens, striking him in the face, flinging her medallion of St. Michael through the doorway, and finally saying "Paddington" to the cabman at dawn—reaches us for the first time piecemeal, tucked without chronological order into the order of Tietjens' long debate with himself.

Ford secures many artistic effects with his use of chronological dislocation: suspense, a lifelike introduction to his characters, dramatic intensity, a meaningful juxtaposition of events. At the same time, by breaking up his narrative within a framework of argument, he establishes an almost continuous contrast between the pretensions of intellect and its achievements. While he reasons sedulously, Tietjens skirts the obvious fact of Sylvia's passion. And Dowell, of course, overlooks practically everything. Their reasoning typically takes the form of dialectic and their dialectic issues in no final conclusions save, for Tietjens, the conclusion that reason itself is inadequate.

The paradox of *Parade's End*—the fact that it is an intellectual novel with anti-intellectual values—is suggestive. Ford's patterns of thought and his intimate sequences of argument are his own creation. Even if they finally serve to show the futility of reason's efforts to solve the important problems of life, do they not at the same time reveal a strong preference for rational order?

The most obvious indication of such a preference is Ford's persistent and eventually successful struggle for moral evaluation of his material. The overall or transcendent dialectic movement of *The Good Soldier* and *Parade's End*—a matter of no single argument but of several and a matter, too, of action, of imagery, of emotional attitudes; in short, of all the ways and means at the novelist's command—offers the evidence for very precise judgment. *Ford's* dialectic achieves in his mature work a full resolution.

There are, however, more particular signs of a fondness for intellectual order in Ford's fiction. The detached narrative voice in Chapter II, Part Two of *No More Parades* places Sylvia's memories and several dramatic scenes within a cause-and-effect sequence; and through his chronological dislocation Ford achieves a firm explanation of Sylvia's behavior. The same penchant for explanation and cause and effect appears in still smaller units of structure. The point of view below is, again, that of the narrative voice (the italics are mine):

> The hansom ran through nearly empty streets, *it being* very early for the public official quarters (*SDN*, p. 10).
>
> Of Mr. Duchemin's curates—he had three of them, *for* he had three marshland parishes almost without stipend, *so that* no one but a very rich clergyman could have held them—it was observed that they were all very large men with the physiques rather of prizefighters than of clergy. *So that* when by any chance at dusk, Mr. Duchemin, *who himself was of exceptional stature*, and his three assistants went along a road the hearts of any malefactors whom in the mist they chanced to encounter went pit-a-pat (*SDN*, pp. 85-86).
>
> Christopher Tietjens—in his shabby khaki, *for* his wife had spoilt his best uniform—spoke suddenly from behind her back. *He had approached her from beyond the pulpit of the two commissionaires and she had been turned towards Mark on his bench* (*SDN*, p. 279).

In *Joseph Conrad*, Ford writes: "The problem of the author is to make his then action the only action that character could have taken. It must be inevitable, because of his character, because of his ancestry, because of past illness or on account of the gradual coming together of the thousand small circumstances by which Destiny, who is inscrutable and august, will push us into one certain predicament."[17] This principle of inevitability Ford sums up under the word "justification," and he credits Conrad with a scrupulous adherence to it. But, really, it is Ford who shows by far the greater disposition to "justify" his events. Explanation and causal relationships figure prominently in *Parade's End*. But in *Nostromo*, as Albert J. Guerard has said, "Life (as form, color, movement) repeatedly reaches us before any coherent understanding of it."[18]

17. Pp. 204-205.
18. *Conrad the Novelist*, p. 175.

Even when the narrative voice in *Parade's End* does not specifically "justify," it still reveals a disposition to reduce experience to
a firm intellectual order, as in the following passage from *Some
Do Not. . .* :

> It was indeed a beautiful room; it had become so during the
> years. It was long and high—matching the Tietjens'. A great
> cut-glass chandelier from the rectory hung dimly coruscating
> in the centre, reflected and re-reflected in convex gilt mirrors,
> topped by eagles. A great number of books had gone to make
> place on the white panelled walls for the mirrors, and for the
> fair orange and brown pictures by Turner, also from the rectory.
> From the rectory had come the immense scarlet and lapis lazuli
> carpet, the great brass fire-basket and appendages, the great
> curtains that, in the three long windows, on their peacock-blue
> Chinese silk showed parti-coloured cranes ascending in long
> flights—and all the polished Chippendale arm-chairs. Amongst
> all these, gracious, trailing, stopping with a tender gesture to
> rearrange very slightly the crimson roses in the famous silver
> bowls, still in dark blue silks, with an amber necklace and her
> elaborate black hair, waved exactly like that of Julia Domna
> of the Musée Lapidaire at Arles, moved Mrs. Macmaster—also
> from the rectory (p. 245).

Order here is largely a function of syntax and cadence. Ford arranges his syntactic units in balanced groups of two's and three's:
"It was indeed a beautiful room; it had become so during the
years"; "long and high"; "reflected and re-reflected," and so forth.
These convey a sense of precision, as does the long periodic sentence that describes Mrs. Macmaster. Order is achieved, too, by
Ford's use of labels or categories. There are the obvious labels of
wealth and culture: *cut-glass, gilt, Chinese, Chippendale.* There is
also the over-all, and satiric, label *traditional,* suggested by the
unifying refrain and by a number of associations which the scene
as a whole arouses. Every item is roundly set in its place, and discredited, including Mrs. Macmaster—also from the rectory. The
narrative style is quiet and exact, a satisfying contrast to the urgent
sequences of thought.

In his article on *Parade's End*, Hugh Kenner praises Ford for
his ability to give "numb counters," like "right," "wrong," "honour,"

and "gentleman," precise meanings. Kenner writes: "'Admirable,' in the first paragraph—'admirable varnish'—is such a counter. It is a recurrent word; and in what novelist but Ford is it anything but a clumsy blur of approval? To have registered a code in which 'admirable' denotes a definite, complex congeries of values is a technical achievement sufficiently astonishing."[19]

The praise is deserved. The phenomenon that provokes it seems, again, to show a fondness for order, particularly for categorizing. Ford's recurrent words and phrases, his leitmotivs, are usually non-objective (they do not, that is, refer to things) and their ordinary, not their Fordian, meanings are vague. As Kenner says, "admirable" is a numb counter—a word in common use with no precise denotations or connotations. Ford proceeds to give it definite meanings of his own. "Admirable" in *Parade's End* signifies well-made, expensively made, designed for display as well as use, designed by and for traditional society, designed, finally, to destroy and be destroyed. Sylvia is "admirably" reckless. Tietjens moves through a series of "admirably" appointed interior settings to the "admirable" trenches of the Western Front. "Game," "parade," "honour," "authority," "control," "proper," "sporting," "circumspect," "correct," and, of course, "tradition," "saintly," and "clean" are also words that recur in *Parade's End* to categorize and summarize.

Conrad and James, to be sure, also use non-objective words and phrases that accumulate meaning from context and serve, as in Ford's fiction, to convey moral evaluations. But such words and phrases play a more prominent role in *The Good Soldier* and *Parade's End* than in Conrad's work or James's. Further, the device appears in Ford's first novel, *The Shifting of the Fire*, when he had yet to experience the influence of Conrad and, presumably, of James as well.[20]

Ford was not, as Edward Crankshaw and Robie Macauley already have noted, a great technical innovator.[21] But he had some-

---

19. "Remember That I Have Remembered," *Hudson Review*, III (Winter, 1951), 605.

20. A source for Ford's use of leitmotivs exists, perhaps, in his own family circle. His father Francis Hueffer, music critic for the *Times*, did much to introduce Wagner to England.

21. Crankshaw, "Ford Madox Ford," *National Review*, CXXXI

thing of his own to say, and he had, too, a distinctive way of saying it. *The Good Soldier* is a masterpiece; *Parade's End* is very, very good. Ford was disposed to reflect a perplexing real world (the world that, surely, most of us live in) and at the same time he gifted his own created world with a tight intellectual and moral order. The complementary concepts of disorder and order by no means exhaust or do justice to his art, but they do seem to provide keys to much that is characteristically Fordian.

(August, 1948), 164; Macauley, "Introduction," *Parade's End*, pp. xvi-xvii.

Epilogue

THIS STUDY has revealed my own preference for happy endings. I have traced Ford's career as novelist through his apprentice work to its successful culmination in *The Good Soldier* and *Parade's End*. But Ford lived, of course, until 1939 and he published five more novels after *The Last Post*. They do not re-create the obscurities and inconsistencies of the novels that antedate the first war. They do, in their various ways, restate the moral and emotional values of *The Good Soldier* and *Parade's End*. Yet even the best of them—even *The Rash Act* (1933) and *Henry for Hugh* (1934)—are not really good fiction. For completeness, however, I shall describe here, very briefly, the final phase of Ford's fictional canon.

In *A Little Less Than Gods* (1928), Ford writes his last historical novel. Choosing Napoleon's return from Elba as public background to a private drama of love, he pursues a typical Fordian theme by discrediting romantic pretensions to greatness. His young protagonist, George Feilding, reveres both Napoleon and the supremely wealthy English sportsman and arbiter of fashion, Assheton Smith. Feilding lives to see Napoleon's triumphant march from the Riviera followed by Waterloo; he discovers that Smith's brilliant social career is founded on vanity and caprice; finally he learns, and this is the major portion of the private drama, that the woman he meets and falls in love with abroad is his half-sister. For his father, too, has lived like a "demi-God"—extravagantly, passionately, irresponsibly.

The circumstances of the hero and heroine are not unfamiliar.

In his preface to *A Little Less Than Gods,* Ford writes: "[This novel] was to have become a collaboration with another writer, but the years went on and [. . .] that writer took on the story alone. But a lamented death cut short his story and I considered myself at liberty to take it on again myself."[1] The writer to whom Ford refers is Conrad; the unfinished novel, *Suspense.* While the main direction of *Suspense* is uncertain—the novel seems barely underway even at the end of its 274 pages—there are many particular resemblances between Conrad's last novel and Ford's last historical romance, resemblances, especially, in the careers and genealogies of both heroes and heroines. Like George Feilding, Conrad's hero, Cosmo Latham, comes from the English landed gentry, has served under Wellington in the Spanish peninsula, has embarked on a tour of Europe, and announces himself an admirer of Napoleon. *A Little Less Than Gods* discovers Feilding already on the island of Elba just before the embarkation for France. Cosmo Latham, at a similar point in history, has reached Genoa, has "half-formed" an intention to visit Elba, and in the last chapter of *Suspense* apparently is bound indeed for the island that harbors Napoleon.

In both *Suspense* and *A Little Less Than Gods,* the heroines are ostensibly daughters of French marquis. They have lived, after the French Revolution, in England; they have been guests, in fact, at the heroes' country homes; and they have been married very young to men much older than themselves, men with new money and new titles. Both heroines have returned to France, then journeyed—one to Genoa, the other to Elba. They don't love their husbands, but have remained faithful to them despite the moral relaxation of the Bonapartist court. Here the quite explicit resemblance between Conrad's Adèle de Montevesso and Ford's Hélène de Frèjus ends. But the implicit one continues. *Suspense* contains a number of hints, so crude as to be seemingly unmistakable, that Adèle is really the daughter of Cosmo's father, Sir Charles Latham. And, though she and Cosmo are not yet in love as *Suspense* breaks off, each has already found the other unusually *sympathique.*

I don't mention these correspondences in order to explore the question of indebtedness. Whether the story of a brother and half-

---

1. *A Little Less Than Gods: A Romance* (London: Duckworth, 1928), p. vi.

sister in love and involved in the destiny of Napoleon's return from Elba was Conrad's or Ford's or, as the preface to *A Little Less Than Gods* implies, jointly evolved, Ford's use of it in 1928, after Conrad had partially exhausted it, signifies, I think, a failure of his powers of invention and a shortage of material.

The problem of mere shortage, he did at least solve. *When the Wicked Man* (1931),[2] *The Rash Act, Henry for Hugh,* and *Vive Le Roy* (1936) all uncover new vistas. They are mainly American and French in setting, in character, and sometimes in idiom as well. Ford's sun and moon now rise over Manhattan penthouses, Hoboken slums, the wide and level streets of Springfield, Illinois, the corridors of the Louvre, and the small, sun-bathed indentations of the French Riviera. His characters suffer the effects of Prohibition liquor, remember meeting Party members in the Village, worry over the decline in Anaconda and Kennecott shares, dance to the music of Russian strings in St. Jean du Var. And yet, Ford's new lode of material is not so much precious as it is plentiful. While it fills four novels, it does not turn round and round in the hand to fascinate and give illumination.

At the heart of the new material lie the old "stories," and they have undergone certain types of change, none of them for the better. As my reference to *A Little Less Than Gods* will, I think, already have suggested, Ford allows the external world to determine the most important actions of George Feilding and Hélène de Frèjus. His nineteenth-century hero and heroine renounce each other; they part in the Closerie des Lilas as Edward Ashburnham and Nancy Rufford part at the station. But the reason for their renunciation is singly and simply an appalling inheritance, no result of their own aspirations and anxieties but of the waywardness of their common father.

When the Wicked Man is a more serious novel. It takes a diffident Fordian hero and looses him, as it were, in a nightmare New York and London world. This world of prohibition alcoholics, bootleggers, molls, and *filles de famille* gone wrong objectifies to the *n*th degree, and encourages, shameful impulses that the hero, Joseph Notterdam, shelters within himself. The situation has possibilities,

---

2. The English edition of *When the Wicked Man* appeared, with minor changes from the American, in London in 1932.

particularly were it all played in some key of anti-realism. But Ford in Nighttown is too often impatient and pedantic. He dogs his hero with a *Doppelgänger*, and then he dogs his reader with insistent stress on the meaning of the macabre visitant:

> [Notterdam] was looking at himself in the dim light and grasped at his hip. He was enraged and determined . . . His other self was a detestable monster: flushed, red-eyed, lecherous, obese, his clothes disordered. You should put a monster like that out of the world he soils.
>
> His gun was out. [. . .]
>
> The other continued to regard him without expression. But his expressionlessness was menacing. He was a menace to the world. To decent men, Notterdam felt that, as against that horror, he was a decent man. Yet they were identical . . . .[3]

The Rash Act, which also presents a fictional cousin-german of John Dowell, offers a similarly bold anatomy of its hero's psyche:

> Over the body of Hugh Monckton, Henry Martin III had eventually triumphed over H.M.A.S. I and II. I, was no doubt the normal Henry Martin of Fall River Psychology: II, which had wanted to take the passport for a lark, was father's product: the child of the wild boar of the Ardennes. [. . .] But Henry Martin III who had eventually won the day had been the acquisitive instinct that was at the bottom of both Luxemburg and Massachusetts—of the cave man that was at the bottom of all types.[4]

A Little Less Than Gods, When the Wicked Man, The Rash Act (and *Henry for Hugh* as well, since that continues the story of Henry Martin Aluin Smith) all point to the same conclusion. Ford is no longer a good psychological novelist. *A Little Less Than Gods* invokes external stimuli to action. *When the Wicked Man* and *The Rash Act*, while they offer familiar Fordian patterns of character, do so by means of oversimplified and hurried statement. And in all these novels, in place of the intricate relationships of *The Good Soldier* and *Parade's End*, Ford realizes only very crudely such

---

3. *When the Wicked Man* (London: Jonathan Cape, 1932), pp. 311-312.

4. *The Rash Act* (London & Toronto: Jonathan Cape, 1933), p. 344.

conceptions as identification and vicarious sacrifice.[5] Notterdam has his Doppelgänger. Henry Martin has a double with nearly the same name, nearly the same face, very nearly the same dissatisfactions and longings.

Ford is often a good raconteur in the novels of his last period. His accounts, say, of the aspirations of the German-born of Springfield, Illinois, or of the clutch of virtues comprised by the French under the word *sérieux,* or of complacent English responses to American gangsterism are amusing and bear witness at least occasionally to sharp observation of the outer world. But Ford has lost touch with the inner world of his best fiction. Certainly in *The Rash Act* and *Henry for Hugh,* his first "story," told to perfection in *The Good Soldier,* loses, like a tale told over again, not its meaning but all its surprises and subtleties. Ford's new French and American material overlies but cannot disguise a fundamental imaginative exhaustion. For reasons a good biographer may some day supply, Ford is no longer intimately involved in his romantic protagonists. Indeed, he seems now to fashion them rather from habit than from any personal need or even interest.

I have said that the moral values of these last novels are recognizably those of Ford's best fiction. Nonetheless, from *A Little Less Than Gods* onward, Ford becomes a sentimentalist, not so much by exalting his protagonists' capacities for heroism or goodness, although he does that in *Vive le Roy,* as by altering their relationships with their worlds. George Feilding and Hélène de Fréjus are the unfortunate pawns of an older generation who have used power, privilege, and wealth irresponsibly. Joseph Notterdam belongs to a society that is even more egregiously corrupt. Both these novels might seem to suggest that Ford was overtaken at the end of his career by pessimism, even bitterness. His sentimentality, his disposition to simplify the complexity of experience, is not, however, of any such consistent sort. *The Rash Act, Henry for Hugh,* and *Vive*

---

5. In this respect, these last novels differ from another rather slight one that Ford wrote between *The Good Soldier* and *Parade's End.* In *The Marsden Case* (1923), rather than debasing the usual subtleties of relationship among his characters, Ford simply sets them off at a distance and concentrates instead, often quite skillfully, on conveying the atmosphere of London just before and during the first war.

Le Roy present heroes who live in remarkably accommodating milieus.

Henry Martin Aluin Smith, like Ford's other diffident heroes, is insecure and inhibited. A puritanical American upbringing has always constrained his emotional life. His wife scorns him, apathetically, and divorces him. His father scorns him, humorously and mischievously, and disinherits him. He is a writer who has never really got down to writing. He is altogether a spectator, loveless, rootless, unemployed. As *The Rash Act* opens, he has resolved to commit suicide. His destiny is not, however, the death by water he so carefully prepares.

The night before he plans to step into the Mediterranean, Henry meets his double, Hugh Monckton Allard Smith. Their resemblance is psychical as well as physical, and Hugh is also keeping a suicide vigil. As chance and some human intervention determine, it is Hugh who takes his own life and Henry who takes Hugh's passport and name. Henry Martin assumes his new identity unconsciously. His quiet sail to suicide meets dramatic opposition in the form of the *trombio*, which wakens his instinct to live, so that he runs his boat toward shore and jumps clear—but not before the boom cracks him once on the forehead, once again on the jaw. Beside himself with pain, Henry Martin races over beach, cliffside, and field until he meets Hugh's lifeless body. He changes passports and staggers on to unconsciousness. He wakes to a world that regards him as Hugh Monckton, war hero, millionaire, and heir to a fabulous English motor company.

There follows, at the end of *The Rash Act* and in *Henry for Hugh,* a long period of convalescence. From the safety of bed and invalid's chair, Henry Martin watches while various tutelaries repair the wrongs and deficiencies of his former life. Hugh Monckton's Aunt Elizabeth serves him, lovingly and gratefully, *in loco parentis*. A passionate meridionale falls in love with him and guards him jealously against unpleasant intruders. Aunt Elizabeth and Eudoxie together contrive to dismiss two disconcerting surrogates for old tormentors—one woman who reminds Henry of a former mistress, and another who reminds him of his wife. Even when Aunt Elizabeth discovers that Henry is not really her nephew, she continues to mother him. She makes him her heir and, we learn when she dies and all is revealed, rightfully so. Henry Martin and Hugh Monckton were cousins. Henry Martin is no pretender, but the legal inheritor of the Monckton fortunes. As the pair of novels ends, Henry crosses the border to Italy and reassumes his own identity. He stands ready to marry Eudoxie, to revisit his American homeland, and, eventually, to assume responsibility for the Monckton works.

The transformation that Ford's first "story" has undergone in *The Rash Act* and *Henry for Hugh* is clear enough. Ford has waved a wand of good fortune over his sun-drenched Riviera to make it a land where all neuroses are cured, all wishes fulfilled. Through an ordeal of pain that is mainly physical and almost entirely passive, Henry Martin's past mistakes and inadequacies are expunged, and he is granted all at once the gift that always eluded Etchingham Granger, George Moffat, Don Collar Kelleg, Robert Grimshaw, and John Dowell—the gift of emotional maturity.

In a mood still lighter than his Riviera one—*Vive Le Roy* belongs generically on the same shelf with Buchan and Ambler—Ford showers the hero of his last novel with blessings even more extravagant than Henry Martin's. Walter Leroy is an American protagonist who does not need the gift of maturity. He is already manly and courageous, able both to work and to love. He possesses, moreover, two august and powerful protectors (one of them is his natural father) who are ready to exalt him to responsibilities greater, even, than Henry Martin's. Walter's double is a king. When the king is killed by Communist insurgents, Walter is first forced, then persuaded, to rule a fictional French kingdom. He becomes a monarch devoted to creating a realm of Fordian ideals—a nation of small producers engaged in craftsmanship and agriculture.

Ford does not take his royal hero and his Utopian kingdom quite seriously—there is evidence of jocularity and self-mockery in *Vive Le Roy*. But this novel of international intrigue underlines the particular kind of irresponsibility that characterizes the fiction of Ford's last period. After *Parade's End*, Ford is no longer concerned to create a credible equivalent of the world we know. He writes sometimes as a pessimist, sometimes as an optimist—and the very inconsistency of his exaggerations suggests, once again, a profound inner detachment. Ford seems to piece his last novels together mechanically, fitting his heroes now with this fate, now that, as if he were a draftsman in Detroit altering old models simply for the sake of variety, simply for the sake of making something new.

His reputation as a novelist rests, and should surely continue to rest, on *The Good Soldier* and *Parade's End*. The novels that precede them prepare for them. And all the novels, before and after, assume various roles in the drama that plays itself out just behind the fictional scene, the drama, of course, of Ford writing his novels.

Index